ZWINGLI THE REFORMER

ANNO AETATIS EIVS XLVIII.

HULDRYCH ZWINGLI
from a wood-cut of 1539

ZWINGLI THE REFORMER
His Life and Work

by

OSKAR FARNER

Translated by
D. G. SEAR

ARCHON BOOKS
1968

*This edition first published 1952
by the Philosophical Library, Inc.
Reprinted 1968 with permission
in an unaltered and unabridged edition*

SBN: 208 00694 x
*Library of Congress Catalog Card Number: 68-8017
Printed in the United States of America*

Contents

Dedicated to
WILLI BIENZ

This book is a translation of the new, revised edition of the work entitled *Huldrych Zwingli, der schweizerische Reformator*, which was published in 1917.

1

CHILDHOOD, BOYHOOD AND STUDENT YEARS

*Use thy youth to advantage! For this time passes
quickly and seldom is it followed by a better one.
No time is more suitable for doing good than youth.*

"I AM a peasant, a peasant through and through "
confesses Zwingli, and he allows himself to be
addressed in Latin letters from friends as "Doggius",
that is, the Toggenburger.* He was born in the
Wildhaus Valley on New Year's Day, 1484, and
baptized with the name Huldrych ; as he never
writes of himself in any other way, he is usually
known by this variation of Ulrich. His birthplace,
situated in the part of the village called Lisighaus,
strikes us to-day as primitive, but for that time it
was imposing ; it has been preserved, and fifty
years ago it was acquired by the East Swiss Protestants for the general public. " A good, old, honourable stock " it was, from which Zwingli sprang.
They had a circular vice in their coat of arms ; the
name of the family may be derived from " Twing ",
i.e., an enclosed Alpine home. His father, like his
grandfather before him, held the position of bailiff
in what was, in those decades, a progressive mountain community. His mother, who was born of the
Bruggman family from the same district, appears to

* The Toggenburg is a valley in the Lower Alps, in the Canton
of St. Gallen. (Tr.)

have been previously married to a native of Thurgau called Meili but evidently she soon became a widow, without having had any children by that marriage. She made up for this by bringing numerous Zwingli boys and girls into the world later ; for eighteen years the cradle was seldom empty. Before Huldrych, came Heini and Klaus ; after him followed Hans, Woelfli, Bartli, Jakob and Andres ; of the sisters we know neither the number nor the names. However did the little brood manage to tuck themselves away in the tiny Zwingli home ? When their witty grandmother had to look after things in the bedroom and the boys protested about the narrow bed, she would perhaps joke about it. The Reformer later related this amusing anecdote in the course of a religious discussion—the Saviour too, he said, must have had to put up with that always with His disciples ; Peter would have come to lie down in front and the Lord would be satisfied with the back place against the wall ; and so when the housewife came to wake them in the mornings she only had to shake the first one awake by a tuft of hair !

Naturally, strict discipline was enforced in the house and the boys were put to work at quite an early age. And it was equally natural that they were brought up under the traditional Church Order. It is true that Zwingli is silent about these matters and does not tell us much about them in after years ; but here and there he lets out odd scraps of information about early experiences. Once, on Ascension Day, he writes somewhere, he and some others had been present in the church when the wooden image of the Risen Christ had been pulled up through an opening in the vault and fruit and sweets had rained down on to the faithful. " What did that mean ? " the children asked the grown-ups. Then it was explained to them that it meant the gifts referred to in Paul's letter : " He gave gifts unto men."

The things he saw in God's world of Nature remained imprinted no less firmly in little Huldrych's memory, especially where the animal world was concerned. He tells the unteachable Luther to consider that the same thing might happen to him as happens to the jay on the lime-twig : " The more he screams and shrieks and struggles in his agitation, the faster he sticks."

Or, another time, when he is urging unity against the common enemy, he uses this illustration : " So also do geese crowd together in a gaggle in order to deprive the eagle of its delight in preying, and so do oxen and harmless sheep make it impossible for bears and wolves to plunder them." And when he wants to impress on people the working of Divine Providence, he recalls how the marmots are warned of approaching danger by the call of their appointed watchman, or how the squirrel sits on a piece of bark and, using his bushy tail as a sail, crosses the stream. Or, when he tries to urge his pastors to discharge their duty faithfully, he does so with an image from the Alpine pastures. " Just as the shepherd strikes some of his sheep, gives others a push or a kick, drives others on by whistling or with salt, while others who are weak he carries or leaves at home till they are strong—so also must God's shepherd deal with his flock in various ways, but always prompted by love." Catastrophes of nature

9

which he experienced also impressed themselves indelibly on his young mind. For instance, the devastation caused by a landslip : " It carries away with sudden violence everything that comes within its reach and uses it to increase its own power. At first it is only the little stones that move ; but their constant impact sets the larger ones in motion, too, until the landslip becomes so big and powerful that it sweeps away everything that comes in its path and leaves behind nothing but wailing and lamenting, nothing but the desolation of the lovely fields and Alpine meadows." Or, if Zwingli wants to represent the blinding effect of false doctrine : " It is the same with our souls as with our eyes ; when someone has been wandering about for a long time in the dazzling snow and then comes to snowless, green places the dazzle still confuses him for a long time ; some people, indeed, have to have medical treatment before they regain their normal power of vision, while others even become totally blind." Thus we see the young Zwingli, in summer and in winter, roving through the meadows and woods and climbing on the mountain slopes, taking everything in with his bright eyes and, guided by his devout parents, already thinking deep thoughts about it all : " There is nothing that would not praise God, not a tiny leaf, not a blade of grass." " Even the gnat would not have its sting and its lovely humming, were it not for the Wisdom of God." And so there may be something true in what Mykonius, the earliest biographer of our Reformer, says, when he remarks that the nearness of the heavens brought young Zwingli, up there on the mountains, nearer to the

Deity, and even in his early days awakened the
god-like element in his nature.

Another gift bestowed by his mountain home and
his birthplace was the fact that from his early days
he was taught to think in terms of the Fatherland.
On long winter evenings, especially, when the family
drew close together in the living room and spent
longer in each other's company, the father, who, as
bailiff, had on his mind the political responsibility for
his mountain valley, would hardly have neglected
to speak of public affairs. There is no doubt that it
was in this way that young Zwingli received his first
instruction in citizenship : he was taught that, even
up there in the Toggenburg, they already belonged
to the Confederation (recently they had joined a
defensive league with Schwyz and Glarus) ; that
they were living in troublous times, when everyone
should be on his guard for the freedom of his native
land. To see this, one only had to look at the brutal
Abbot of St. Gallen who was trying to diminish the
hereditary rights of the miners ; but it was particularly evident when one considered the intrigues of
those who, for the sake of foreign gold, drove the
much desired Swiss mercenaries to enlist in foreign
armies. Added to this, was the fact that growing
tension with their neighbours on the other side of the
Rhine was making itself felt more and more threaten-
ingly until it exploded in the Swabian War. Thus the
Zwingli boys were committed to follow the example
of the great Swiss heroes, such as William Tell, the
" hero strong in the strength of God and first
instigator of Confederate freedom ", and Nicholas of
Flueh, who " spoke solemnly of a Confederation :

11

that it could be conquered by no master or force but only by self-interest ". And they may have been told in enthusiastic terms of the victorious battles of their ancestors, who risked their blood and their lives for the Fatherland, as, for example, the one " at Naefels in Glarus, where three hundred and fifty men one day repeatedly attacked fifteen thousand and, at the eleventh assault, put them to flight . . . as a result of which the idea of a Confederation won praise in every land ". And so it was important to be a brave Swiss even from one's childhood days—others will come and spoil the dear homeland. Then, in the spring, when the south wind swept the meadows free of snow, the band of boys and young men wanted to start active training for the Fatherland. They practised running, jumping, putting the stone and fencing; and woe to anyone who raised any opposition and spoke scornfully of the Fatherland ! Zwingli confesses later : " Even as a child, if anyone teased us Confederates and upbraided or slandered us, I resisted them and even ran into danger on that account ; for anyone who dishonours the Confederation also dishonours me."

He may well boast of his love, " which, God knows, all my life right from childhood I have borne for the good Confederation with such steadfastness and determination that even in my early days I practised all sorts of arts and worldly wisdom in order to be able to serve it ".

But how would he do this ? What sort of a man would he become ?

Huldrych had an uncle on his father's side, called Bartholomew, " a devout and renowned man " who from 1484 to 1487 was assistant priest in his home town of Wildhaus and then became parish priest and dean at Wesen on the lake of Wallenstadt. It was to him that the first schooling of his clever nephew was entrusted. In May, 1529 Zwingli writes in the foreword of his Commentary on Isaiah that he began to learn early, that he had already been a student for forty years. Thus in 1489, in his sixth year, he must have gone over the Height of Amden down to Wesen, where he was to stay for five years, living in the parsonage by the parish church at Otis, primarily to learn Latin. Then, when he was only ten, he went to Basle. His new teacher, only about — six years older than he, and himself still a young student, was Gregory Buenzli from Wesen, hence known to Zwingli's uncle ; all the more readily did the latter hand over to him the inexperienced high-school boy. Now in Basle there began the so-called " Trivialschule " (primary school), whose main task was the perfection of the Latin language. One had to be so far advanced in it that one could talk in Latin to the masters as well as to one's comrades—any other language was forbidden ! Later, Zwingli mentions somewhere the school-book he used at that time, the so-called *Cato teutonice expositus*, in which the German translation was printed in the spaces between the lines of Latin—an amusing crib which goes to show the mechanical methods of language teaching used in those days. It is not possible to ascertain now whereabouts in Basle Zwingli lived at this period. All we do know is that he made excellent progress (in music as well, for which he had a remarkable gift from the very beginning) and even surpassed some of the older students.

After about two years, when the good Buenzli had finished his Latin, Huldrych went from Basle to Berne in order to " matriculate " there, as we might say to-day, at the Humanist school of the famous scholar and poet Heinrich Woelflin (Lupulus). And so, probably living with relatives in Kessler Street, he continued his studies in this " town of the bear " for another two years, in the school close by in Herren Street, where the casino stands to-day. In Berne his lovely voice nearly decided his fate : the Dominican monks tried to entice the musical lad into their monastery and they were beginning to succeed ; he had actually written home to say that he was starting his noviciate. But, in spite of the fact that they were good church people at Zwingli's home, both father and uncle were averse to papal desires ; they immediately imposed their veto and called the young boy home without delay, soon after which they sent him to Vienna to attend the University.

Now this was certainly a different sort of thing from monastic life, living and studying in a way incomparably more exposed to the world, and enjoying the world. Ancient and modern literature, history of olden times and peoples, but especially worldly wisdom, above all that of the Greeks and Romans, were taught and learnt here. " They must first of all acquire philosophy and fine culture ", writes Zwingli fourteen years later in the letter of introduction with which he, in his turn, sends two students to Vienna. Zwingli's name is found twice in the college register (1498 and 1500) ; the first entry is deleted and someone has written *exclusus* (expelled, turned out !) in the margin. Perhaps the fiery Swiss had rashly got himself involved in political discussion and fallen out of favour for that reason (it was in the middle of the Swabian War) ; or perhaps, and this is more likely, an enemy of Zwingli had first deleted his name irregularly. However that may be, for the rest of his life our Reformer remained grateful to Vienna for the rich profit he acquired there in the course of four years.

Then, from 1502 to 1506, followed his second stay in Basle, where he now brought his studies to a close for a while. In 1504 he obtained his Bachelor's Degree and in 1506 he became Master of Liberal Arts (which would be roughly the equivalent of " Doctor of Philosophy " to-day). At the same time, the student was acting also as a school-teacher at the Church School of St. Martin, and already his innate aptitude for teaching was becoming evident, for fifteen years later a petty sessions clerk from Urn thanked him for the instruction he had received from him and confessed that, although he had meanwhile forgotten his Latin, he always liked to go back in his thoughts " to the well from which sprang so much delight in the heat of my childhood ". And for Zwingli too, on his part, the intercourse with young people may have supplied the refreshing influence he needed ; for the college, with its scholastic pressure usual in Basle at that time, was not always adequate to satisfy his heart, hungering as it was for joyful activity. Fortunately he found, outside the University, contact with a small circle of progressive Humanists (including the printers Amerbach and Froben and their proof-readers), with whom he liked to spend a refreshing social evening, sometimes joking merrily, sometimes enjoying serious music, sometimes discussing the latest books. It is quite probable that the thought of the goal of his studies, the priesthood, rather oppressed Zwingli, who was barely twenty-two at this time. For his theological tutors were not particularly inclined to make ecclesiastical work seem attractive ! He probably suffered from time to time from the feeling that the two things did not go well together ; one should be either a humanist or a theologian, either a scholar or a clergyman. When he went into the theological lecture-rooms, he felt himself, according to Mykonius, " nothing but a spy in the enemy camp ".

Then, in November, 1505 Thomas Wyttenbach from Biel came to the college as a teacher and it was to this man, as clear-sighted as he was unassuming, that Zwingli owed the growing realization, just before it was too late, that humanism and theology should go together, that is, that the humanistic method could be profitably applied to the study of the Early Fathers and the Bible. Only for a matter of six months was the Toggenburger (together with Leo Jud from Alsace, who remained a lifelong friend) allowed to sit at this scholar's feet, but he never forgot how, under his guidance, he began to free himself " from the empty chatter of the sophists ". Had it not been for this, he might never have become even a Roman priest, to say nothing of anything greater.

16

2

Truth is for me what the sun is for the world. Just as we greet it with joy wherever it may rise, so the spirit too longs for the light of Truth and rejoices wherever it finds its beams.

AT the age of only twenty-two, Zwingli was ordained priest. His uncle in Wesen had probably smoothed his nephew's way to Glarus, which was seeking a new pastor, and arranged things so that the Toggenburger received preference over another applicant. At Rapperswil, on the Lake of Zurich, where Zwingli had a relative who was a priest, he preached a trial sermon and in his home church at Wildhaus on Michaelmas Day he celebrated his first Mass ; then, from the end of 1506 until the autumn of 1516, he was " parish priest of Glarus ", as the official title ran.

As well as the market town itself, three neighbouring villages were included in the same parish—a third of the whole canton—certainly a full, heaped measure of work for a beginner. But the lively young pastor was not lacking in readiness for action and he immediately won the confidence of the flock entrusted to him. As a priest who was patriotic in the best sense and as yet, of course, completely loyal to the Pope, he looked after his people and mastered his daily duties. He also set to work with a will for the extension of the church ; under him the building was enlarged considerably by the addition of the so-called Chapel of the Cross.

In addition to his manifold official duties, in which he had a few assistants, he managed to find time, astonishingly enough, for other things ; for here he zealously continued his humanistic studies. Without becoming by any means a learned stay-at-home, he devoted his leisure time—it must have been the hours of darkness more than anything else—to a thorough study of literature, in which he was interested. But he did not read only theological works and certainly not only dogmatic literature of *one* school of thought—from the very beginning and right to the end his principle was : don't be partial and don't become narrow-minded ! Pick out the best from all sides ! Don't sell yourself completely to anyone but learn something from everyone ! And this gave a rich quality to his thinking and an unusual breadth to his education. In his own private library one could already see a most varied selection of works. In the summer of 1510, for example, he ordered from Cologne Ptolemy's *Geography*, Aristotle's *History of Animals* and the works of the Italian philosopher Pico della Mirandola ; the lofty train of thought of the latter particularly bewitched him. In order to be able to read the Early Greek Fathers in the original text, he mastered the Grammar of Chrysoloras and later asked his friend Vadian, who was then a celebrated Professor in Vienna, for further aids : " for so firmly have I resolved to learn Greek that no one but God can deter me from it ! "

In addition to this, he also gave lessons to young men of Glarus and, in the school which he founded, prepared them for the University, especially the sons of the noble family of Tschudi, among them Aegidius, who later became a historian, and his cousin Valentine, who was afterwards his successor in Glarus. And, when they went away, he still remained tutor to these students and guided them so that they did not "stick too long with those studies which I was too late in shaking off". In a lively correspondence, he supervised the course of their studies and their moral conduct. During the holidays he placed his books at their disposal and, in high spirits, played the lute and the trumpet with them. In overwhelming gratitude they called him "the most zealous protector of science", "the model of fine and learned culture", probably also "Aristotlean", and compared him, because of his intellectual wealth, even with Apollo, while they normally addressed their letters "to the philosopher and theologian Zwingli".

It is difficult to say what was the tone of his pulpit preaching at this time : for not a single sermon manuscript from the Glarus period has been preserved. But one of the earliest of Zwingli's literary efforts, dating from the year 1510, has come down to us in poetic form under the title : "Fable of the Ox and the other Beasts, coined for present events." Guess what I mean, he exclaims : An ox, grazing in an Alpine meadow, is ambushed and decoyed by all kinds of animals, a lion, a leopard and a cunning fox ; with smooth words each one tries to win him over to his side as an accomplice. Look out, warns Zwingli, you splendid steer ! Stay in your own meadow and feed yourself honestly ! For this fable concerns the national danger of enlisting mercenaries for foreign service, and anyone who means well for the homeland should give the warning and spoil the devil's game which the foreign enlisters are playing ! The lion is the German Emperor, the leopard, the King of France ; the fox, Venice, but the watchful dog represents Zwingli himself.

> Garden of Peace, thou Alpine field,
>   Of thee will I sing and relate.
> Here mountain peaks watch o'er thee keep
>   And there do the mad, rushing streams.
> In the green clover grazes nearby
>   The young, sturdy bull, russet-hued,
> Wide-set his horns and curly his brow.
>   From chin and from neck drooping down,
> Down on his broad and massive chest,
>   His paunches fat and heavy—
> Picture of power and blissfulness !
>   And then, if attacked by thirst, the beast,
> Snorting, would sip from the icy rill.
>   Yet did it please
> The granter of these wondrous gifts, suspecting
>   All and hating
> All whom Fortune favours, to mix,
>   With the sweetness, gall . . .
> But faithfully there follows fast
>   Behind the bull the watchful dog ;
> He scents attack from fearsome foes
>   And warns the steer, who is his friend.

" Seest thou the approach of cunning beasts ?
    Then stamp thy feet
With forcefulness ! We needs must call
    Upon our friends,
Who, as protecting spirits, guard
    Our Fatherland.
To them we should devote ourselves
    Anew, with faithful heart " . . .
" Leave me in peace ! I'm grazing the clover,
    And scorn your words."

Thus one can see what a keen interest the priest of
Glarus took in political events. The patriot in him
opposed the venality of the Swiss. And this attitude
was only strengthened when he came to see the
horror of mercenary war at close quarters. Twice,
thrice did he accompany the warriors of Glarus to
Lombardy as their chaplain, and thereafter he
appealed for peace with increased determination
and urged the maintenance of strict neutrality :
" One should not actively support any party, let
princes be princes and let us remain Confederates !
Hold together and let foreign lords squabble among
themselves, do not hire yourselves out so that you
receive all the blows they would inflict on each
other ! " Enlistment in foreign armies is moreover
" the school of all vices and the mother of troubled
consciences ". After all, one need not be ashamed
of the homeland on account of its poverty : " She
may not produce cinnamon, malmsey, oranges,
silk and such feminine fancies but she does produce
butter, milk, horses, sheep, cattle, home-spun cloth,
wine and corn in abundance." And on religious

21

grounds, too, war is already rejected on principle not from God, but " from us come wars ; if we spent as much trouble on the arts of peace as we do to promote quarrels, things would be all the better for us"

Zwingli received his most lasting shock from his experiences in the murderous Battle of Marignano. In vain did he call upon his disunited Confederates, a few days beforehand in the Town Hall Square at Monza, to stand together ; and, even after 6,000 of them had been left behind on the battle-field, the lesson had still not been learnt, and not a few of them proved ready to become involved once again in an alliance with foreign masters. Then Zwingli put pen to paper again—it was at the turn of the year 1515/16—and wrote a second, more fiery, political poem ; *The Labyrinth.* And in this Cassandra call, too, the powers of the world are again alluded to in animal images : this time the poet represents the Pope by the lion ; the Emperor, by the eagle ; France, by the cock ; Venice, by the winged lion ; and all kinds of satellites, by the gods. For the divided Confederates, Zwingli introduces the images of the ox and the bear, the former representing the Eastern Cantons surrounding the Uri Bull and the latter representing the Western Cantons under the leadership of the Bernese Bear, which is led by the nose-ring and dances at the will of its French drover. But how we should interpret Theseus, who passes the frightening pictures and penetrates into the depths of the labyrinth, where he kills the monster Minotaur, and Ariadne, the daughter, who with her thread enables Theseus to find his way through the maze—

all this is explained by Zwingli in the moral at the end, in the following words :

Listen then, my people dear,
  What signifies the labyrinth here :
It is the world's distress and woe ;
  Whilst Theseus, the brave hero,
He is the strong and pious man
  Who always righteous actions can,
And for the Fatherland is strong,
  For it alone. The beast denoteth wrong
And sin and shame. Whereas the thread
  Means reason, by which is said :
Who'er with honour would come through,
  Must always righteous paths pursue.
And Ariadne represents
  Reward of virtue none resents.
See now the deeds of all mankind !
  They act as though they were quite blind
And in the labyrinth roam about
  Without a thread and can't get out
Again to light of day ;
  They wander round and lose their way . . .
If with our God our trials we'd share,
  They would not be so hard to bear ;
But nought within our hearts doth burn
  Whereby we all vain things might learn
To scorn as dirt, and thus ensure
  The certain help of God. Wherefore
The world is full of faithless arts,
  For Christian love rules not our hearts,
But in its place are pagan ways
  And even worse. Oh, what a maze !

23

For pagans act most cautiously
   In all their undertakings. But we,
With all our pride and skilfulness,
   Go rushing round and make a mess
Of all we do—whence comes our plight.
   For he who brutally can fight,
Is held by all as brave and bold.
   Is this what we by Christ were told ?
Nay, He did teach, while on this earth,
   That he alone doth prove his worth,
Who for a friend his life lays down.
   But look how we, for mere renown,
Do risk our lives ; for selfish ends
   Most grievously we hurt our friends.
We seek to gain our fame and glory
   By stupid wars and battles gory
And every natural law transgress
   By conflict, strife and bitterness ;
As though to this our earth to-day
   The Furies fierce had found their way,
Let loose from darkest depths of Hell.
   What have we Christians then to tell
Of Christ ? His we are in name alone ;
   Our works, they are the devil's own.
In none is love or patience left.
   Our rulers, they are quite bereft
Of Christian love of any kind.
   For, if on aught they set their mind,
To fight for it they will not cease.
   And when God mercifully sends Peace
To shine on this our land so dear,
   We more like beasts than men appear !

Now this poem—one might even call it a sermon—was not actually printed but became known in Glarus probably only in manuscript form. But that sufficed to make the parish priest, who probably sounded the same note now and again from the pulpit, disliked by persons of authority. In short, the zeal with which Zwingli endeavoured to thwart the renewal of the alliance with France, which had expired in 1515, unsaddled him and cost him his position in the land of Fridolin. " I have indeed ", he writes afterwards from Einsiedeln, " taken a strong interest in public affairs and, as a result, have suffered, and learnt how to suffer, much hardship." The French party had brought about his downfall and compelled him to move into the " dark forest ", where good friends found him another sphere of activity. But for the following two years he still remained in name the priest of Glarus ; the majority of his parishioners there, being well-disposed towards him, probably hoped they would get back their brave shepherd when times became more peaceful. But man proposes, God disposes.

Later on, Zwingli often referred to the year 1516 as being particularly decisive for his development ; it was then that he began to preach evangelically. The world-famous Humanist leader, Erasmus of Rotterdam, was among the first to assist him in this. It all began with a hymn by this master, which came to the notice of the priest of Glarus as early as 1514 ; in this was shown, with overpowering clarity, how all our running after the peace of Heaven ends in blind alleys ; for there is no other

DESIDERIUS ERASMUS
Engraving from a painting by Holbein

Saviour but Jesus alone. And before long we find Zwingli making a pilgrimage to Basle, where the great scholar was now living and working, and being greatly pleased by a personal talk with him. It is almost impossible to get a clear conception of what Erasmus meant to him from now on ; he probably never admired any man to the same extent as him whom he praises as " the most learned of all scholars ". Erasmus certainly became *the* experience of the two years at Einsiedeln during which, less disturbed from without, he was able to deepen his own culture. The prior of the monastery and his friend, Frank Zink, also contributed to this happier state of affairs. It was here, in the monastery at Einsiedeln, that Zwingli studied the New Testament in the Greek edition of Erasmus (this new publication, of great importance to him, had reached him when still at Glarus) and from this he copied out Paul's Epistles, word for word. As soon as any new work of Erasmus was printed, his friends and publishers in Basle had to send it to him here immediately. From here he followed unremittingly Erasmus's personal fortunes and the ever-widening circle of the movement he started, and, every time his followers reported on this, the bearer of the letters, the lame Andreas Kastelberger from the Grisons, had to cart parcels of books to Einsiedeln, principally the Early Fathers, Jerome, Ambrose and others, but also secular writers. Zwingli himself confesses how at Einsiedeln he " studied with unceasing vigour, day and night, the Greek and Latin philosophers and theologians ".

There is no doubt about the fact that Zwingli,

27

having embarked on this course, partly of his own
accord and partly at the instigation of Erasmus,
had already become much more of a theologian
than he was in Glarus. More and more he withdrew
himself from those dissolute Humanists, whose
ambition it was " to be followers of Catullus and
Propertius, rather than followers of Paul and
Christ ". *Christian* Humanism was now the theme,
" philosophy of Christ " was the watchword. People
expected nothing less than a return of the times of
the Early Christians ; " Renaissance of Christianity " was the scholarly slogan for it, which
recurred again and again in the letters. From now
on, Zwingli began to make sound criticism of the
existing defects of the Church, especially its venality
and doctrine of justification by works (in Einsiedeln
there was no lack of material for this). From here
too he made a laughing-stock of Bernhard Samson,
who, in 1518, was boldy offering indulgences for
sale in the neighbourhood of Einsiedeln. Others,
too, ridiculed the indulgence-sellers, it is true ; but
it seems that Zwingli already had a deeper perception
of the truth and was taking what he had learnt
from Erasmus more seriously than was the latter
himself, who, though toying with new ideas, was not
yet ready to be taken seriously. Various signs
point to the fact that, in the latter part of the
Einsiedeln period, an increasingly decisive and
clearer note was becoming perceptible in Zwingli's
preaching, to the joy of the one side and the dismay
of the other. People said he should be warned
against going too far where the monks were concerned ; but, as it happened, these were among his

supporters. The Papal Nuncio in Switzerland got wind of the danger and hastened to decorate him with a special mark of honour ; he was named the Papal Acolyte and with that fine title was bound more closely to the Church. And the clever Cardinal Schinner von Sitten—they already knew each other from Marignano—took an interest in the case and thought he could tame the agitator with fine eulogies and promises. But all this labour of love was in vain. The pure Word of God had already penetrated too forcefully.

In October, 1518 the office of secular priest at the Cathedral in Zurich became vacant, and immediately people thought of Zwingli, who was already widely known for his eloquence and his political attitude. After he had given reassuring information on account of certain false steps, and had beaten, not without a certain amount of bad feeling, a rival competitor, " the Swabian dog ", he was elected on the 11th December by a majority of the Zurich Chapter. After having finally renounced his office as priest of Glarus, he arrived on the 27th December " honourably and well-received " in the Limmat town.* On New Year's Day, 1519, a Saturday, and his thirty-fifth birthday, he mounted the pulpit of the Cathedral for the first time and immediately surprised his congregation with the declaration that he now intended to take no notice of the appointed Scriptural readings but to preach right through the Gospel of St. Matthew from A to Z. And the next day he began with the first chapter, explaining to his listeners what the Biblical narrative has to tell

* The Limmat is the river on which Zurich stands. (Tr.)

us about the genealogy of the Son of God. No one suspected yet that, with this new man, they had handed themselves over to a Reformer ; the thought that this was what he must become even took his own breath away. But, in his very first year at Zurich, God granted him the experience which made him into one.

3

I am the clay ; mould it to perfection or else destroy it.

IT was a strange coincidence that Zwingli, in those very days when the prospect of being elected to Zurich was keeping him so much in suspense, began to take an interest in Luther. And now it was the Wittenberger who strengthened the Toggenburger and acted as the backbone of the final venture. At the beginning of December, 1518 Luther's name appeared for the first time in Zwingli's correspondence, and, in the course of the next few years, it was to re-appear more frequently than that of anyone else. The reason for this was that the book-sellers of Basle were not only bringing Luther's writings on to the market but were actually printing copies themselves, to the special joy of the Humanists there, who welcomed Luther as a comrade-in-arms. Here indeed was what they themselves were seeking, but Luther was already expressing their ideas with greater decision and force ! And it was for the same reason that Zwingli, too, joined in the general enthusiasm for Luther. In actual fact, he did not find in Luther very much that he had not known before ; rather did he stretch out his hands to Luther now because the latter became for him a welcome confirmation of what he himself had discovered. There was no doubt about the fact that people would be all the more ready to accept Zwingli's discovery, when a spokesman of Luther's calibre was supporting his evidence. And so it was partly due to Zwingli that, throughout the town and district of Zurich too, Luther's works were sold from house to house ; and, even from the pulpit, he recommended their reading (especially the Lord's Prayer and the penitential Psalms, as well as the edition of the " German Theologia ").

But the thing that did most to win him over was the report of Luther's brave attack at the Leipzig Disputation, which reached his ears in the summer of 1519. Councils here, councils there—but even they may be wrong ; the Holy Scriptures alone are infallible, and their message is that salvation can be attained even without the mediation of the Pope ! The fact that anybody had dared to express this view in public must have been an amazing experience for Zwingli. Years afterwards he still praised and thanked his Luther for this : in the days when the others (he includes also himself) had not yet plucked up their courage to take up their stand against the giant Goliath (i.e. the Papacy), " then you alone were the courageous David who with well-aimed sling smote his gigantic body to the ground. It was you who brought about the fall of the Roman boar ! " And it is clear that in those weeks after the Leipzig Disputation, when the revolutionary action of Luther, whom the people of Zurich were now welcoming as the returned prophet Elijah, was making its influence felt over in Switzerland, Zwingli, with trembling heart, began to understand what the mission of a Reformer might

MARTIN LUTHER
from an engraving by Daniel Hopfer

entail. He asked himself where it would lead to and where it must end if he, too, now let himself be dragged out from the study of cautious considerations into the storm of reckless realities. Was he to do it ? Could he achieve it ?

And now he won his spurs through unexpected trials : he fell dangerously ill. The plague broke out in August 1519 ; Zwingli, who was having trouble with gall-stones again, was at the time taking the waters at Bad Pfaefers. Responding to the call of duty, he immediately hurried back to his congregation and did all he could as a fearless minister, not sparing himself, risking his life every day. How frightful was the epidemic is seen from the fact that, during the six months in which it was raging in Zurich, about 2,500 people fell victims to it ; and the significance of this is only clear when one realizes that at that time the town numbered only 9,000 inhabitants. It was a decimation worse than that of the most gory war. In September of that year, it attacked Zwingli too ; for a time he hovered between life and death. In Basle and Constance people were already mourning his early death ; they said that now their finest hope was destroyed and the best preacher taken from them. All the greater was the rejoicing when, at the beginning of November, it became known that he had passed the crisis. But, as a convalescent, Zwingli had a bad time ; for a long while he suffered from fatigue and had to go on dressing his wounds until the New Year. Even after that, his memory was not up to its previous level ; he was still convalescing by the following summer. There is no question that the experience of the plague deepened Zwingli's character and, in the end, made him more resolute. We learn this from the song, finely polished and equally mature in form, content and melody, which, after his recovery, he put down on paper and set to music :

AT THE BEGINNING OF THE ILLNESS

Help, Lord God, help
  In this distress !
I think that Death
  Is at the door.
Come, Christ, before !
  For Thou hast conquered Death.

To Thee I call :
  Be it Thy will,
Pluck out the dart
  That wounds my heart.
Allow me not
  One hour of peace, to pause for breath.

And if Thou yet
  Wouldst have me dead,
Amidst my earthly days,
  Yet may I still Thee praise.
Thy will be done !
  Nought can me stun.
Thy tool to make
  I am, or break !

For takest Thou
  My spirit now,
From earth away,
  Thou dost so, lest it go astray
And others' state
  And pious lives contaminate.

85

IN THE MIDST OF THE ILLNESS

Comfort, Lord God, comfort !
  The illness grows ;
I am in throes
  Of agony and fear.
Therefore draw near
  To me, in grace and mercy.

Thou dost redeem
  Him who can trust,
As all men must,
  And his hopes place
In Thine own grace,
  And for Thee all else set aside.

Relief has come ;
  My tongue is dumb,
I cannot speak one word.
  My thoughts are dark and blurred.
Therefore 'tis right
  That Thou the fight
Shouldst carry on
  For me, Thy son.

I am too weak,
  Dangers to seek ;
Nor can I fight
  The devil's taunts and evil might ;
Yet will my soul
  Be Thine for aye, complete and whole.

IN CONVALESCENCE

Healed, Lord God, healed!
I do believe
The plague does leave
My body now.
And lettest Thou
The sinners' scourge depart from me,

Then shall my mouth
Through all my days
Show forth Thy praise
And wisdom more
Than e'er before,
Whatever dangers may beset me.

And though I must
Become as dust
And suffer death, I know,
Perhaps with greater woe,
Than did befall
And me appal,
As I did lie
To death so nigh,

Yet will I still
My part fulfil
In this our world
And all things bear, for Heaven's reward,
With help from Thee,
Who art alone to life the key.

And it was after this experience that, for the first time, Zwingli's preaching reached the heights of absolute clarity and determination. This can be verified by a roundabout method. When, in 1520, he was preparing a lecture on the Psalms, he wrote numerous notes in the margin of his Psalter, and these very entries show beyond dispute that the writer had come to acknowledge completely the ideas of the Reformation, that is to say the fundamental Pauline conception of the justification which God grants in Christ. And he makes no secret of the source of this basic discovery ; he had been studying the works of Augustine, especially his interpretation of St. John's Gospel, and, in this way, had come to a complete understanding of Paul's doctrine of salvation. And it was only after this that he became fully conscious of his mission as a Reformer ; it was like a flash of lightning and one can hear the thunder in his letters of those months. For example, the one dated the 24th July 1520, when he comes to the following conclusion : " As for me, I am, by this time, quite prepared for evil from all sides, clergy and laity. I ask for one thing only : that Christ will enable me to bear all things with manly heart and that he will shatter me or make me whole, as He pleases, for I am His implement. If I am excommunicated, I will remember Hilarius, who was banished from France to Africa, and Lucius, who was expelled from his seat in Rome and then returned with great honour. Not that I would make myself equal to them, but I would be solaced by them : for they were much better than I, and nevertheless had to suffer so much which they did not deserve. And if ever I should boast, then may it be with great joy, only because I have had to suffer shame for Christ's sake."

It was part of Zwingli's cautious peasant nature that, in everything he did, he set to work with great care ; there was nothing he disliked more than rushing into things heedlessly and dashing at things impetuously. First of all, he took plenty of time, and *thought* what he wanted. Only then, when he was quite sure about it in his own mind, did he *say* what he wanted. And again it might be quite a time before he *did* what he wanted. On New Year's Eve, 1519, summing up, as it were, his first year at Zurich, he had written to a friend : " In Zurich, there are already over two thousand more or less enlightened people who, hitherto, have only been feeding on spiritual milk, but soon they will be able to digest solid food." After the middle of 1520, it seems he no longer minced matters ; what he said after this was the authoritative word of the Reformation.

He was in the pulpit every day, as it were ; naturally, there was no opportunity for detailed written preparation. He had to manage with brief notes, which he jotted down and took with him into the pulpit. Nevertheless, he always had an apt expression on the tip of his tongue. And everything was so clear and amusing, no affectation, no pathos, nothing stilted about his preaching ; no special cassock was put on, no special pulpit voice affected. Foreign words he could not abide ; his dear mother tongue seemed to him so beautiful and so rich that he did not understand those who wanted to adorn it with other plumes. He wiped the dust off the Bible and translated the old expressions so cleverly into the current language of the day that it was understood and indeed often found amusing. He did not hesitate to introduce a joke now and again at an appropriate place—may nothing worse ever happen in the Cathedral than that occasionally someone laughs !

Nevertheless, every time Zwingli mounted the pulpit steps, he realized that it was a matter of dealing seriously with the most serious of all subjects. That was his office and his holy passion : the revealed Truth must be cleansed of the addition of all human wisdom (and stupidity !) ; the overgrowth of alien ideas must be cut away until the Word of God could be heard without distraction. " Woe unto them ", he proclaimed in the church, " who want to twist the Holy Scriptures to suit themselves ! May thunder and hail come upon them ! " Naturally people tried to restrain him. " Don't be so outspoken ! Be more docile ! " the cautious ones warned him. But he replied : " Do you really consider my words to be too harsh for our human depravity, which shrieks to high heaven ? If the preacher is not allowed to proclaim the Truth, then let a lute-player or bagpipe-player mount the pulpit ; we should all like listening to that, and everybody would be happy."

No one could think more highly of the priestly vocation than did Zwingli ; he had before him the ideal of a prophet who will not let himself be led astray to right or to left, but proclaims the naked Truth (God's Truth) and works passionately so that the will of the Master may be done. And though from time to time he spoke of the beauty of the priesthood, saying for example : " No greater happiness can come to a man than when he is privileged to cast the nets of the Lord ", nevertheless this feeling was not uppermost in him ; on the contrary, the sense of responsibility involved in this mighty task oppressed him. " Even in my early days ", he confessed, " the priesthood gave me more anxiety than pleasure, because I have always realized that the blood of the lambs, which are lost as a result of my neglect, will be demanded of me." But he could do no other : " When a lion roars, who will not be afraid ? And likewise, when God prepares the way for His Word and proclaims it, who will not hear and follow it ? " " God now sends His Word, that it may heal. We see the splendour of His Word so clearly and powerfully that we have the sure hope that the Spirit of God will liberate the people just as well to-day as when it led Moses out of Egypt." " The Word of God will take its course as surely as does the Rhine ; one may dam it up for a while but cannot stop its flow ! " This faith in the penetrating power of the Word of God was, at that time, a revolution for the world. In fact, it remains the greatest miracle that the town of Zurich has ever experienced ; for twelve years, Zwingli went on preaching the Word (by 1525 he had preached right through the New Testament) and, by the end of that time, there had been accomplished the most momentous change that ever took place within its walls.

4

*It looks as though it will be fulfilled, as it is written :
The rulers take counsel together against the Lord
and against His Anointed. Grant, O Lord, that they
may be confounded and that Thou, with Thy Word,
alone shalt conquer ! Amen.*

THE Word he proclaimed met with a ready
response ; it was amazing how Zwingli's preaching caught on and stimulated to action both friend
and foe. People said they had never heard anything
like it ; those who had not been near the church for
years now attended regularly. For instance, there
was the treasurer Raeuchli, whose favourite remark
was that, at the Council of Constance, some thousand
priests had met together and the most pious one of
all they had burnt to death—he was referring to the
Czech, John Huss. Then there was the bell-founder,
Hans Fuessli, who, on hearing Zwingli's first sermon,
commented : " He is not going to mince matters ",
and, from then on, because he was hard of hearing,
was always to be seen on the left, below the pulpit,
with his hand to his ear.

Not all, however, were equally edified immediately.
But that was only as it should be ; for " The Word
of God must meet with resistance in order that its
power may be seen ", as Zwingli himself asserted.
To begin with, he came up against the canons of the

Cathedral, because, from the pulpit, he disputed the divine institution of the tithe. People tried to point out to him that he should not say all these things in public at once, but such remarks carried no weight with him now. " The Word of the Bible must prevail, whether it suits us or not." In May, 1521 the Conference of Lucerne authorized the King of France, in case of war, to recruit up to 16,000 Swiss mercenaries. Then there occurred what previously had been considered impossible : Zurich refused the alliance with France. And one man alone had tipped the balance ; it was Zwingli, who later explained the miracle in these words : " No other weapon in Zurich has rejected mercenary warfare, but the Word of God alone." Meanwhile, with less success but with no less violence, Zwingli was raising his voice against the propaganda of the Pope ; against his agents, for example, he hurled these words which might have come from one of the Books of the Prophets of the Old Testament : " Rightly do they wear red caps and cloaks ; for, if they are shaken, ducats and crowns fall out of them and, if one squeezes them, the blood of sons, brothers, fathers and friends flows forth."

Then, in the early spring of 1522, there arose the first friction with the Bishop of Constance. In spite of the fact that it was Lent, people were eating meat, in the house of the printer Froschauer amongst other places, in Zwingli's presence. As this caused a stir and incurred penalties from the authorities, the Reformer expressed his opinion about it in one of his sermons. This was something so unheard of that the Bishop grasped the opportunity of admonishing the rebellious Zurichers to be more obedient towards ecclesiastical laws. But Zwingli did not have to waste much time with the suffragan Bishop Fattli, who appeared with a couple of other gentlemen in the Limmat town ; for the Council stood fearlessly by its secular priest, who was under attack. Zwingli now printed an amplified edition of his sermon under the title " Concerning choice and freedom of food, of offence and defilement", his first work as a Reformer. In its content, it was the counterpart to Luther's *Liberty of a Christian Man*. If people want to talk about offence, he said, then let them do so ; only let us be clear who it was that first gave offence, namely the Papal court, which, contrary to the Gospel, imposes on Christian people intolerable burdens in order to earn money by their fasting. " If you want to fast, then fast ! if you don't want to eat meat, then don't eat it ! but leave me, as a Christian, free to go my own way ! "

Both sides now received reinforcements : Zwingli gained a powerful supporter in Leo Jud, who came to St. Peter's in Zurich from Einsiedeln, where he had succeeded Zwingli ; the Bishop of Constance also gained support from the diocesan chancellor, Faber, who had just returned from Rome as a firebrand. The conference declared itself adaptable to the wishes of the Bishop and shut up the priest of Fislisbach, who had been swayed by Zwingli's doctrine, in the prison of Baden. Zwingli, meanwhile, addressed the people of Schwyz in a letter, attempting to persuade them to follow the example of the people of Zurich and forbid mercenary warfare, since all warfare was unchristian, however

LEO JUD (1482–1542)

Zwingli's friend as a student in Basle and later
his fellow-campaigner in Zurich

much one tried to disguise it. In July, ten of the Schwyz priests showed that they, too, had been personally influenced by the Word of God : in a petition to the Bishop and the Federal Estates, they declared that the celibacy imposed on them was an intolerable burden on their conscience, and asked to be relieved of this impossible condition. " Have mercy on us, ye faithful and willing servants, and grant that that which is not sinful in the eyes of God shall neither be shameful in the eyes of men." If this plea fell on deaf ears, more success was achieved in the conflict with the monks. It was no wonder that their bitterness against Zwingli was boundless ; their reputation had not exactly improved since he had made an exhibition of their ignorance and laziness, both in the pulpit and out of it. But, when they tried to induce the Council to forbid any polemics against them, and the Council showed itself inclined to submit the dispute to a court of arbitration, Zwingli invoked his right and his duty before God : " It is I who am bishop and chief priest in this town of Zurich and it is to me that the work of minister is committed. It is I who have taken this oath and not the monks ; it is not for them to supervise me, but I them, and if they preach what is not true then I will oppose it, even if I have to go into their own pulpit and talk against them." And he was right : the Council ruled that henceforth evangelical preaching should be allowed even in the monasteries.

Zwingli now published three main works, following quickly one after the other. The first of them, the *Archeteles,* was to have been the " beginning and end ", the first and last word between him and his opponents. The basic idea of it was : God's Word above all ! The Bible, the canon of all faith and life ! For the Bible is the oldest and the purest authority ; ecclesiastical tradition is unnecessary. The power of the Pope is of later origin ; the enforced celibacy of the priests is a transgression against Scripture ; Councils, compulsory fasting and indulgences are innovations and, therefore, false. People immediately raised the following objection against Zwingli : that is all very well, but people like us cannot understand the Scriptures ; we need someone who will give us certain guidance and definite interpretation of them : the Early Fathers or the Councils or the Pope. To this Zwingli replied with a printed sermon : *Of the clarity and certainty of the Word of God,* which he had first preached to the nuns at Ostenbach : there is no need for Councils or Popes, for " The Word of God is a bright light and does not let people go astray in the darkness ; it teaches itself, reveals itself." The only condition for this is that one shall not violate the Word of God but, in places where it appears to be obscure, light it up by clear passages of Scripture. In the third publication, the sermon entitled : *Of Mary, the pure Mother of God,* Zwingli rejects the calumny that he was denying the immaculacy of the Virgin Mary. This deals a blow to the myth of the cool, too sober manner of Zwingli ; for here he strikes the warm, heart-felt notes, almost like a mediaeval mystic !

There had been an uproar because Leo Jud had interrupted a monk, while he was preaching in the

47

Augustine monastery. Zwingli took advantage of this in order to carry out a plan he had long cherished, that is, to get a decision on the points at issue by means of a public discussion on religion. Friends and foes, including the episcopal curia in Constance, were invited to the Zurich town hall on the 29th January, 1523. As a basis for the arguments to be carried on there, Zwingli composed his *Sixty-Seven Conclusions*, which show how thoroughly he had already thought out the Reformation to its consummation. The first fifteen state the positive doctrines : what the Gospel is, who Christ is, what the Church is. " The sum of the Gospel is that our Lord Jesus Christ, the true Son of God, proclaimed to us the Will of His Heavenly Father and, by His sinlessness, redeemed us from death and reconciled us to God." With the sixteenth thesis, there begin the relentless negations : the Pope, the Mass, the intercession of the Saints, good works, compulsory fasting, pilgrimages, the vows of the monks, the celibacy of the priests, gabbled prayers, indulgences, confessions, works of repentance, purgatory, ordination of priests—all these come hurtling down. With victorious logic and wonderful frankness, all are attacked, even the wielders of worldly power : " In so far as they rule unfaithfully and fail to uphold the Christian ethic, may they be deposed in the sight of God ! "

Of the six hundred men who came to the Council Chamber of Zurich early in the morning of the appointed day, the majority were clergymen from all over the Canton of Zurich, but there were a few from other parts ; from Constance there came the

diocesan chancellor Faber, " in his red soft hat "
(his doctor's cap), with a few satellites. Zwingli sat
in the centre at the front, with the Hebrew, Greek
and Latin Bibles open before him. The Mayor of
Zurich, Röist, opened and led the discussion. The
Bishop's spokesman, Fritz von Anwyl, was the
first to take the floor : he said he had really come
only as an observer, to ascertain on the spot which
way the wind was blowing, down there in the
Limmat town. Zwingli then rose—there were many
who saw him that day for the first time : a rather
slender man of medium height. No well-groomed
beauty was he and yet there was something strangely
likeable in his innate strength and freshness. His
eyes, intent in their gaze, and yet joyful as they
looked around. Deep forehead, thick neck, some-
what protruding chin. His movements, measured
but definite. His voice, clear but not too strong.
And so he presented himself to anyone who found
anything heretical in his *Conclusions*, ready for
question and answer : Well now, here I am, in the
Name of God !

Thereupon, Dr. Faber, evasively : " As has
already been said, we do not intend to enter into
disputes ; that is what the universities are for,
there is Paris, Cologne or Lyons." But he does not
get away with this ; Zwingli calls across to him :
" But what about Erfurt ? Wouldn't you consider
Wittenberg ? " " No, Luther would be too near ",
replies the chancellor of Constance. They laugh
and jeer. Zwingli gives them to understand that the
tailors and cobblers of Zurich now have as much
right to talk on biblical questions as high-school

teachers ; proudly he points out that this gathering is quite in a position to decide matters ; there is even an impartial judge—and he lays his hand significantly on the Bible. The mayor exhorts everyone to express his own opinion and, when there is silence, Zwingli asks " for the sake of Christian charity and truth ", why he is reprimanded as a heretic. But none of his opponents has the courage to speak. Someone calls out to the meeting from the door at the front, " Where then are the clever Dicks who make such a brave noise in the streets ? Step forth now ! Here is your man ; you can probably all talk over a glass of wine, but here no one will utter a word ! " But they merely beat about the bush and get nowhere.

Then the Pastor of Neftenbach rises and asks why the bishop had imprisoned his colleague of Fislisbach, to which Faber replies that the latter was an ignorant man and that, with the aid of the Scriptures, he had easily convinced him of the error of his opinions on the Saints and the Mother of God. Thereupon Zwingli demands to know what were the relevant Biblical passages. But the clever gentleman turns round and cannot submit any proof for all his fine talk, so that the mayor says mockingly, " The weapon, with which the Pastor of Fislisbach was stabbed, cannot be produced ! " Eventually they commence discussion on the real points at issue, first the question of marriage of the priests, then in the afternoon, Faber having at last read Zwingli's Conclusions in the lunch interval, they come to the question of Church tradition and the Mass. Again and again Zwingli has to ask his assailants for the relevant passages of Scripture, but all in vain. Faber demanded adjudicators for the Word of God ; the Reformer remained adamant about his slogan, " The Word of God is self-evident." Again and again he urged that anyone was at liberty to refute him, but only with " Scriptural evidence".

It is no wonder that Zwingli's cause won the day ; the opposition was, indeed, weakly represented. The Council reached this decision : Master Zwingli shall continue to proclaim the Holy Gospel, as hitherto, according to the Spirit of God, until such time as he be instructed by a better authority ; and, likewise, shall all the other pastors preach in their parishes only that which they can uphold by genuine divine Scripture. By the people's will, therefore : Zurich is to be Protestant ! When the decision was read out, Zwingli, deeply moved, exclaimed : " God be praised and thanked, for His sacred Word shall prevail in Heaven and on earth ! "

In the course of the next few months Zwingli was engaged on his most comprehensive and most significant Reformation work, written in German : *Interpretation and substantiation of the Conclusions.* If anyone wants to sound the depth and fullness of Zwingli's thought, to see the power of repartee and the assurance of victory of this fighter—here he will find both, almost better than anywhere else. Here are a few examples : " Just as the iron of the plough is not the work of the hammer but of the smith who made them both, so also do our works and we ourselves come of God, who made the works and us, His tools." " Just as the Spirit of God is never lazy or idle, but is eternally working and creating, so is

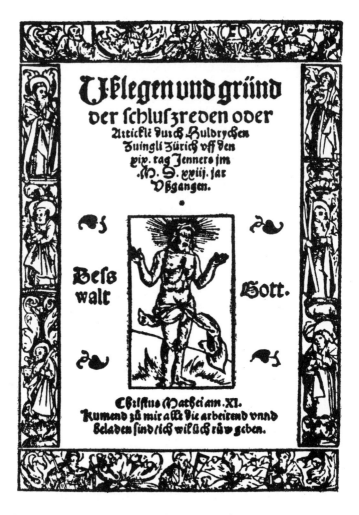

TITLE-PAGE OF ZWINGLI'S BOOK

Interpretation and Substantiation of the Conclusions,
printed by Christoph Froschauer in Zurich, 1523

it equally impossible for a good man to be idle."
" If you want to belong to God, commit yourself to
His care, let Him hold sway and give you life, sus-
tenance, counsel and all things ; then will God live
in you." " This might be the prayer of the farmer
at the plough, doing his work patiently in the Name
of God, calling upon God to swell his grain and often
considering that this earthly life is nothing but
misery and woe, but that in the life beyond the
eternal Goodness will give us rest, peace and joy."
" No greater encumbrance ever came upon Man
since the world began, than the great lazy crowd of
hypocritical clergy, popes, monks and nuns." " It
is faith, not confession that makes a man pious. He
who rightly believes, will confess to God every day
of his own accord, as often as he sins." " We have
such a heap of idols : some we clothe in coats of
armour, like mercenaries ; others we dress like fools,
no doubt in order to attract women to worship.
The women (*i.e.*, the images, representing the women
saints) are fashioned so luxuriously, sleekly, and
painted as though they were put there for the very
purpose of inciting lasciviousness. And thus we probably give ourselves pleasure and think we are
having a lovely service, when it is really nothing but
idolatry." " What indeed would Amos, the peasant
prophet, say, if he were to witness the many kinds of
music, with its trills and lively dances, in our temples
and, in between, the young canons in their silk
surplices going up to the altar to sacrifice? Devotion
does not parade itself before men, but seeks quiet-
ness." " Regret not the murmured prayers of the
temple. But hail to thee, thou devout, innermost

prayer that is aroused in the heart of the believer by the Word of God, be thou nought but a feeble sigh! Hail to thee, thou family prayer, that all Christians use for one another, whether it be in the temple or in one's own chamber, so long as it is free and without gain!" "A clergyman should not be recognizable by his tonsure and his clothing, but by his love for all men, his sympathy in their need, his zealousness in the preaching of the Word of God, and his readiness to help, wherever he is needed." "The doctrine of God does not descend from the high and mighty ones, but it grows up from the humble and despised to the high and mighty." "Therefore should all governments, however small, be vigorous and undaunted; as long as they hold to the teaching of Christ, God will not let them fall."

In the same year, the question of the images of the saints had to be settled. Could they still be retained, after people had been convinced by the new preaching that there was no Biblical foundation for the adoration of them? On the one hand, not a few people felt themselves conscience-stricken; on the other hand, the Council still felt bound to take steps to punish those who, on their own responsibility, removed crucifixes, altar-tables, etcetera from churches or public places. Thus, at Zwingli's instigation, a second religious discussion was announced to take place on the 26th October, 1523, again in Zurich town hall. Not one of the bishops who were invited attended the meeting, but Zwingli found no difficulty in consoling himself for their absence: "Hoengg and Kuesnacht constitute a church more surely than the whole body of bishops and popes."

There appeared only about 350 pastors from Zurich and the surrounding districts, and also about a couple of hundred laymen. On the first day, they dealt with the images, on the second and third, with the Mass. Zwingli's bravest ally, Leo Jud, denounced the " idols ". He used the Old and New Testaments as his witnesses and wanted to make a completely fresh start, even demanding the removal of the images hanging in private houses. Superintendent Schmid, of Kuesnacht, represented a milder point of view. On the second day, the debates were still more violent ; each pastor was called upon by name and asked for his opinion. The pastor of Glattfelden said, amongst other things, that he was of the opinion that the country was better off before Hebrew and Greek had been discovered. Then Zwingli raised his finger scoldingly and called across to him : " Herr von Glattfelden ! one can see from your tail what sort of a bird you are ! " Even now Superintendent Schmid showed himself as the most broad-minded and tractable ; from the other side, Hubmeier, Stumpf and Grebel, the young Baptists, were pressing for ruthless and rapid advance. Fundamentally Zwingli agreed with them ; but for tactical reasons he still held back. No decision was taken ; it was left to the authorities to discover ways of carrying out, at the most opportune moment, what was recognized as the truth.

On the morning of the third day, Zwingli delivered the most powerful sermon that has been handed down to us from him—called " The Shepherd "— in which he confronted his colleagues with the picture of the true evangelical preacher and pastor.

Independence of family and relatives is the first condition for anyone who will venture to become a preacher of the Word of God. And, whatever he teaches in words, he must prove by his actions. Like the ephors in Sparta and the tribunes in Rome, shall the pastors look after their congregations; like the prophets of the Old Testament shall they fight as knights, ruthlessly, in spite of death and devils, in the service of their Master. " Fearlessness is your armour ! You must watch and be ready for battle ; for God sends His prophets everywhere to warn the sinful world. The less you fear death, the stronger is your faith. The more you fear death, the less confidence and divine love is in you. Where there is true faith and divine love, then does a man know that to die in God's service is profitable and the beginning of the true life. . . . And afterwards he will give thanks unto God, because He has seen fit to use his mean body for His honour. May He draw you into knowledge of Him, so that you may be humbled under His powerful hand and the Cross of Christ and be blest with all believers ! Amen. " That was demanding a lot, indeed ! The goal was a high one. We understand that the young Thomas Platter, hearing a similar sermon of Zwingli's, had the feeling that someone was pulling him up by the hair and that he came to the conclusion : " If that is how things are, then good-bye to the priestly state (presumably : evangelical priesthood !) ; I will not be a priest any more." But Zwingli lived out this prophetic ideal, to the encouragement of his friends and in defiance of his enemies. In him there weighed now the inexorable spirit of Elijah. Ahab and

Jezebel, indeed, were missing in his Zurich. In the Council he had an ever more willing helper. And the people answered only " Yes " to the great levy.

5

The true believer is he who looks unto God alone, leans upon Him alone, depends on and trusts in Him alone, hopes in Him alone, takes refuge in Him alone and knows that he can find all his needs in Him alone.

IT was an hour of supreme importance in the history of Zurich, as the realization now dawned that the time was ripe, that the old order must pass away and a new reality appear ! It is said—and not without reason—that Zwingli was so deeply moved by the issue of the second Disputation that, in his final speech, he proclaimed, in a voice stifled by tears, " Do not be afraid, my friends ! God is on our side and He will protect His own. You have indeed undertaken something big and you will encounter much opposition for the sake of the pure Word of God, which only a few bother to think about. Go forth in the name of God ! "

But it was just at this time that there began also the awkward difference of opinion with the Anabaptists. " All the earlier battles were child's play compared with it ", Zwingli confesses, and this had a profound influence on the practical effects of the Reformation regarding Church organization, Radical followers of Zwingli, at first called " spirituists " and led by Konrad Grebel, Simon Stumpf, Balthasar

Hubmeier, Felix Manz and Wilhelm Roeubli, accused the Reformer of going too cautiously and stopping at half-measures. They said that the time had now come when they ought to be taking the Bible seriously in its full literal meaning : that the life of the congregation ought to be reorganized to follow exactly the pattern of the time of the Apostles, i.e. the responsibility of the layman, the priesthood of all believers and the pooling of possessions ! " Be rid of the State," they said, " and let us have a Free Church ! Above all abolish infant baptism ! only adult baptism has any biblical foundation ! " Zwingli realized immediately where this radicalism must lead : to sectarianism and the undermining of all civil and ecclesiastical authority. It is understandable that he therefore opposed it most resolutely. It must not happen that the truth of the Word of God, which was coming into circulation again, should be choked by the cramping influence of conventicles. " If it should come to pass that every hot-headed crank should form a new group as soon as any new or strange idea came into his head, there would soon be so many sects that, in every parish, Christ would be divided into numerous pieces."

His quick perception of this danger now, for the first time, really strengthened the churchman in Zwingli, who saw that the best guarantee for the maintenance and expansion of the Protestant Cause lay in a firmly founded people's national Church. His estrangement from these enthusiasts took on literary form in his comprehensive writings entitled : *Of baptism, anabaptism and infant baptism.*

Of the preacher's office, and also in his work : *A true and reasoned answer to Dr. Balthasar's book on baptism*. But he expresses his most fundamental views on this subject in his extended sermon : *Of divine and human justice*. In this he said : " The contemporary State does not, of course, correspond to the ideal of Christianity, but we are living in a world in which, for the time being, there can be nothing but half-measures. Only by unwearied and persistent preaching will we be able to approach slowly the high goal. And the authorities themselves should play an active part in this work of educating the people ; by virtue of the office which God has bestowed on them, it is their duty to rule, to ward off sin by their laws, and to promote amongst the citizens readiness for mutual help. The Church may confidently go hand in hand with the State ; so long as there is a Christian authority, which submits to the authority of the Biblical law, one need fear no wrong development." One can see what confidence Zwingli had in the State and he was not disappointed in this, for down in the Town Hall they were aiming ultimately at the same things as up in the Cathedral : the supremacy of the Word of God concerning justice and grace.

At the end of 1523 began the reorganization of the church service ; until then almost everything had remained outwardly the same as under the old order. Zwingli's principle in these reforms was : First of all, be law-abiding ! " Do not do anything behind the backs of the authorities and on your own responsibility ! " Secondly, be thorough ! For " if you do not destroy their nests, the little storks will return." In the town itself and in most of the villages, there was no question of " iconoclasm "; rather was everything done in accordance with the decrees of the authorities. Those who had their own images standing or hanging in the churches might take them away ; in this way a lot of them disappeared. In the municipal churches, men set to work, under the orders of the Council, in June, 1524: the three secular priests, Zwingli, Engelhart and Leo Jud, two constables and an honourable master craftsman from every guild, and, finally, the municipal master builder with his locksmiths, stonemasons, carpenters and handy-men. They shut the doors from the inside and removed all the decoration that had now become superfluous ; ladders were placed against the painted walls and all the splendid colouring was either scratched away or whitewashed over. Now Zwingli was able to rejoice : " Our temples in Zurich are indeed light ; the walls are beautifully white ! "

And in other respects, too, the former ceremoniousness was replaced by a sobriety hitherto unknown ; the canonical prayers and the sung matins and vespers were no longer heard ; no song resounded now through the sacred building ; the organs remained for a while unused and then, finally, were removed. The same Zwingli who confesses somewhere, " It is strange that none of the arts is so closely related and bound up with the human spirit as is music ", did not lift a finger to give his congregation the evangelical hymn. They should now have an ear for one thing alone : the Word of God. But there were purges in other respects too : the monstrances and other gold and silver equipment used in worship were melted down ; the ecclesiastical vestments were sold or removed ; the relics were done away with ; in the Cathedral, the bones of the local saints, Felix and Regula, which previously had been preserved so reverently, were " buried honourably and quietly ". No longer did incense rise up to heaven ; no longer were banners and crosses carried in procession in the streets. It was already being said, " Let the people keep their images and colourful splendour ! " To which Zwingli answered : " God does not want to be honoured with outward show, but with faith, love and purity, in spirit and in truth . . . Christ commanded us to teach not by images but by the Word." He went on to say that God's true images were men, especially the poor, for whom we should care ! What did it matter if henceforth things looked much less pious, if the monks " let hair grow over their bald heads ", if the monasteries emptied and became instead poor-houses and hospitals ! When Zwingli came to Zurich there were ninety-two secular priests, thirty monks and ninety-two nuns ; when he died there remained only three secular priests, with a number of assistants. But, whereas the former had previously spent their lives as parasites, the latter now shouldered a heavy burden of work. For now there was a sermon every day, generally twice a day, and on Sundays there were also special services for children and for servants.

The keystone of the innovations in worship was introduced on Maundy Thursday, 1525 ; then, for the first time, instead of the Mass, Zwingli celebrated

the Lord's Supper according to biblical custom.
First of all, from the pulpit, he summed up what he
had long been teaching on this subject : Away with
the bloodless repetition of the bloody sacrifice on
Golgotha ! The Supper was instituted by Christ,
so that we might remember His act of redemption
with special praise and thanks and be stirred to more
complete obedience and more faithful service to the
brotherhood. Finally, away with all the magic that
had been carried on long enough with the holy
symbols ! Bread remains bread and wine remains
wine. What good would it do us even if we could,
outwardly only, taste with our lips of the body and
blood of the Lord ! If there were no faith the most
eager eating and drinking would not help one jot.
It is faith alone which can provide meat and drink
for the soul. It is the spirit that quickeneth ; the
flesh profiteth nothing. Are you serious about it ?
Are you worthy of this partaking ? To be worthy
does not mean to present oneself without sin ; if
that were the case, no one would be able to come.
He is worthy of the Lord's Supper, who knows his
own unworthiness and calls to the Saviour : " Lord
be merciful to me, a sinner ! "

And now the Reformer leaves the pulpit and comes
down into the body of the church. There stands a
simple table, over which is spread a linen cloth and
on which are placed the Communion vessels, everything as plain as possible, without any show, no
silk or silver or gold, the dishes and cup made only of
wood. With a few assistants, Zwingli now stands
at this table and, with his face turned towards the
congregation, begins to pray, using only the German

63

language, so that he can be clearly heard and understood. Then, in turn with two deacons, he reads out the Liturgy with the Biblical account of the Institution. And, when they have themselves partaken of the Bread and the Wine, they go with the vessels to the congregation ; from pew to pew they hand the sacred symbols to the people. First the Bread—it was unheard of and had never happened before: they take it themselves from the dish, break a piece off for themselves and then pass the rest on to the person sitting next to them. Then the Cup with the Wine : for the first time since this Cathedral was built has the command of the Master been obeyed within its walls : " Drink ye *all* of this." Having returned to the table, Zwingli now prays, using the 113th Psalm, and then dismisses the faithful with the impressive injunction that they must now go out and fulfil the word of reconciliation in their lives. " Lord we give Thee praise and thanks for all Thy gifts and blessings, who livest and reignest, God, world without end." Thereupon the deacons respond : " Amen ! " And finally, Zwingli : " Go in peace ! "

Shortly afterwards he wrote to a friend about this first Communion : " The number who partook of it was greater than I have ever seen before and the number of those who looked back to the flesh-pots of Egypt was far less than I expected." And later he wrote somewhere that, in Zurich, they had experienced how the communal celebration of the Lord's Supper had become a power for peace ; members of the congregation who had been living in enmity, now came and, as if by chance, sat down next to each other, and, having passed the Bread to each other and drunk of the same Cup, found that they were able to conquer their hate and forget their quarrel.

It was natural that one of Zwingli's main concerns was the training of an efficient clergy. In April, 1525, he became Principal and set to work eagerly on the long-prepared plan for the reorganization of the Cathedral College into a theological training establishment. The aim of the college, from the beginning, had been improved training of the clergy, and therefore, he inferred, its income was to be used in this way in the future. His experiences with the Baptists had also convinced him that the training of the theologians must be as thorough as possible, especially from a linguistic point of view ; he did not want preachers who were sectarians or laymen at the job, but men who were well equipped scholastically. By the middle of June, things had progressed far enough for the " Prophecy " to be put into action. By " Prophecy " he meant the study in the minutest detail of the Holy Scriptures, under the guidance of spiritual tutors, for prospective preachers and those already holding office, who were to form the nucleus of a theological faculty.

Every day, except Sundays and Fridays, at seven o'clock in the morning during the summer (eight o'clock in winter), all the pastors, canons and students would gather together in the Cathedral choir and sit down in the pews there. First of all, Master Huldrych steps up to the lectern and prays for the guidance of the Holy Spirit ; then he steps aside and beckons to another. The latter opens the

Bible ; his task is merely to read the text for the day, in Latin ; the Book he holds in his hand is the Vulgate. And when he has finished his passage, he is relieved by a third, who places a folio volume, the Hebrew Bible, on the lectern ; the Hebrew scholar deals with the same passage in this version. After him there follows a fourth, who reads the same extract from the Greek of the Septuagint and elucidates the meaning from this. A fifth explains in Latin how this portion of the Word of God should be utilized for a sermon, while a sixth, sometimes Zwingli himself, sometimes one of his colleagues, takes over the preaching in the German language of the passage which has been studied so thoroughly, thus benefiting also other listeners who have meanwhile assembled.

These efforts, spread over many years, culminated in the Zurich Translation of the Bible, to which Zwingli himself contributed a good part. He was an artist in language and could knock the nail on the head when it was a question of making Biblical expressions comprehensible to the simple man. For " Priest and Levite ", in the Parable of the Good Samaritan, he suggests " parson and clerk "; for " if the salt has become dull ", " if the salt has lost its savour ", and so on. And he finds many expressions which sound a homely note in the ears of the Swiss, as, for example, at the beginning of the 23rd Psalm, which he translates, " The Lord is my Shepherd, I shall not want. He makes me rest in lovely Alpine pastures."

But Zwingli considered a thorough revival in the whole life of the people as no less urgent than the reorganization of Church forms ; and, in face of the new radiance of the Word of God, the dark gloom of social evils could no longer be tolerated. The peasants' revolts of 1525 showed him, more clearly than he already knew from his own home and from his experience in the Glarus district, where the shoe pinched for the country people ; the evils of the town he knew, by this time, from his own observation. However much his sense of loyalty to the State may have urged obedience to the authorities, one nevertheless gets the impression that, in his heart, he was on the side of the oppressed and those who were deprived of their rights. It was him, indeed, they had to thank for the abolition of serfdom and the relief of the tithes ; and it was he who, from then on, repeatedly impressed on the pastors that they should not preach the will of God only with words but that they should look after all those who were at a material disadvantage and relieve their condition, as far as was in their power. " I will have nothing to do with the covetousness and insubordination of the peasants, but one must not treat them too harshly "; this is Zwingli's standpoint in these matters. The social side of his work is seen also from the fact that it was under his leadership that the poor relief was put on a new footing. Hitherto the poor had existed for the Christians (so that the latter might help them and thus earn a place in Heaven) ; now the Christians were to exist for the poor (in order that they might raise them up from the mire, instead of prolonging their beggarly lives by almsgiving). And, whereas hitherto charity had only been a matter for the individual, it was now to be the concern and duty of the State and of the Church.

Zwingli easily found the means for this ; again and again he pointed out that the goods presented to the churches and monasteries belonged to the poor, and the poor-law decree of January 1525 gave effect to this. As long ago as the beginning of 1524, the " poor-house " had been set up in order to enforce, by positive means, the prohibition of the degrading practice of street-begging ; soup and bread had been handed out every morning to all " paupers ", in what was hitherto the preacher's monastery and, thus, care was taken that no one who had fallen upon hard times through no fault of his own should starve and become demoralized. Even the poor and needy were to learn that the message of the Father's mercy, revealed in the Son, which was being proclaimed with new tongues, was no empty phrase.

Furthermore, in May, 1525, new marriage laws were passed, whereby the jurisdiction in matrimonial affairs, which, under existing Church law, was a matter for the Bishop, was now transferred entirely to the Zurich Council. The ecclesiastical court in the town and the so-called parish-boards in the country had to keep watch over propriety and morals and to punish sternly adultery and prostitution. Strict mandates were promulgated against the vices and exuberances that were in vogue and, in the end, these mandates even laid down regulations for social intercourse, dress and public amusements. Careless blasphemy, dice and card games, the wearing of silver and gold jewellery, velvet, silk and low-cut shoes, the " disorderly, impure pastimes " of Shrove Tuesdays—all these were forbidden. And the curfew was legally introduced by the great moral mandate of the 26th May, 1530 ; none of the indigenous population was to be seen in the evening " after nine o'clock " in public-houses or club-rooms ; and, after that hour, no innkeeper was allowed to sell wine to be taken away, except for " sick persons and women in childbed ". In those days, there was no toleration of the contradiction between pure teaching and impure living ; no one would be content with an appearance of piety. And the rules had to be followed in the daily business of life : " Whereas the divine Word has been accepted, every devout man must exert himself to the utmost to adhere to the divine Word in everything, not only by words, but by works."

The only danger was that such an authority might become tyrannical and might intervene in matters where State coercion had no place, as, for example, regular attendance at divine services was ordered by the State or when the authorities used forceful measures against the superstitious, as happened with regard to the Anabaptists : Hubmeier was tortured, Felix Manz was drowned in the Limmat (and died unflinchingly). And measures were taken also against the Catholic remnant of the population of Zurich, with unchristian severity. One must not pretend that Zwingli was an upholder of modern freedom of conscience ; when it was a question of organizing and governing the Zurich State Church, his natural love of power became evident. Nevertheless, we must admire him for his acute perception. He saw that a

State Church was now simply a historical necessity and that in it lay the only guarantee for the continued existence of the new faith. The future proved him to be right : without the strict State Church Order, the Reformation everywhere would have been in danger of being lost in either fanaticism or legality.

6

THE OPPOSITION OF THE CONFEDERATES

He who takes care and does not make his move without due deliberation, he is the one who wins the game. Care and deliberation win the victory.

ZWINGLI was never a mere local patriot ; from the very beginning, he was concerned with the whole Confederation and the goal he pursued was the furtherance of the new movement, until it affected the whole of Switzerland. Almost every page of his correspondence after 1520 bears witness to this fact. He made full use of his old friendships and cultivated new ones to enable him to work to this end. At first there was considerable hope ; everywhere there were Confederates who could not escape the wonderful magic of this newly-discovered Gospel ; and, if to begin with they were numerically only minorities, they would certainly become majorities as soon as the clear Word of God had been proclaimed for any length of time. That was what Zwingli anticipated. Thus, certain of victory, he imagined that his Zurich experiences would be repeated throughout the Confederation. So, with increasing resolution from year to year, he pressed for permission for the evangelical sermon to be preached in every canton throughout the Fatherland ; everything else would then follow automatically. There were, however, two factors to which he had not given sufficient consideration. First, the long-standing bad feeling of the provincial cantons against the towns, which received new nourishment at the first sign that recent events in Zurich might shift the centre of influence to the disadvantage of the country cantons. Secondly, the uncanny power of personal calumny ; for how could one pay any impartial attention at all to the new preaching when its instigator and chief representative was slandered, from the very beginning, as a " Lutheran knave " and when, in the Forest Cantons as early as 1522, taunts like this were made from the pulpits : " The Turk is on our doorstep and anyone who can carry a stick or stave should march out against him." The fact that the Confederal Disputation, which Zwingli suggested as early as 1523, did not materialize is greatly to be deplored ; an open discussion face to face might have been able to nip in the bud many a personal and factual misunderstanding.

The opposition on the part of the Confederates became more violent in 1524 ; now they did not hesitate to represent the " idolators' war ", which was going on in the town and district of Zurich, as an act of violence against the Christian Faith itself. So great was the animosity that already people wanted to exclude Zurich from the Confederacy. But Zwingli's opponents were divided among themselves and, as a result of this, the decision was postponed ; and every year of delay spelled additional strength and extended conquests for the Reformation. Nevertheless, in the Federal Assembly, which incidentally had not met in Zurich since the 13th March, 1522, there was already talk of having

Zwingli arrested, because his preaching was the cause of great confusion, as well as all the dissension. And the seriousness of the position is evidenced by the imprisonment of the Zurich iconoclast, Hans Hottinger, who was seized by the bailiff in Baden and beheaded in Lucerne. The Bishop and the Papal nuncio exerted pressure ; as a result of this, the strictly Catholic Cantons, Lucerne, Zug, Uri, Schwyz and Unterwalden, joined together in a separate league at Beckenried in the April of 1524.

Both sides continued to add fuel to the fire. On the one side, there was the carrying-out of the Reformation in the Zurich village of Stammheim, which in the matter of " criminal offences " came under the jurisdiction of the Confederation ; and the burning, by an excited mob, of the Ittingen Monastery, to which a Protestant parson had been enticed by night by the Catholic bailiff of Frauenfeld. People thought they were on the eve of war ; therefore, in spite of all Zwingli's opposition, Zurich gave way and placed the under-bailiff of Stammheim, Wirth, who was not guilty of the uproar, and both his spiritual sons, together with Ruettimann, the bailiff of Nussbaum, at the disposal of the Federal Assembly which was meeting in Baden. As a result, three of them had to pay for this incident with their lives. There was great bitterness in Zurich, where a " secret Council " was now appointed, which in these days of great tension was to hold its meetings behind closed doors and take the necessary precautions ; Zwingli himself belonged to it and surely not as a silent observer ! At that time (December, 1524) he was also planning his first " Counsel ", that is, a plan of war, on which he had bestowed great care and put down on paper in all haste. Like an experienced general, he was already envisaging an attack in grand style : negotiations were to be sought with foreign powers and a rebellion to be let loose in the Tyrol against the Emperor ; detailed instructions concerning armament, the chaplain, and the trumpet signals were given. Authoritative rules of conduct for the senior military officers were distributed : they must be God-fearing and not self-reliant and must regard the confidence of their subordinates as their highest treasure, " not to disdain them but make them obedient, nevertheless, and to esteem them as one of yourselves ". Here we have the patriot again, but he is one who is already reaching out beyond his own frontiers and venturing to raise all the forces of the world for the sake of the Word of God.

On the other side, too, foreign politics played their part and, in this case, it was not merely on paper. The Bishop of Constance and John Eck, the old opponent of Luther, succeeded in annexing the Catholic Cantons to the Regensburg League, which had been formed after the Reichstag of Nuremberg as a counter-thrust against the Lutheran movement in Germany. As early as October, 1524, Austria and the Federal Assembly had almost come to the point of binding themselves to mutual support in matters of faith. But this proposal fell through again, for the time being, after the Battle of Pavia ; the sight of the returning mercenaries, thoroughly exhausted after fighting in the service of France against Austria, did not exactly encourage war in their own country. But Zwingli, nevertheless, remained awake and sought new alliances ; he wrote to the Rhaetian League at Muelhausen. When, in 1525, the High Mass was abolished in Zurich, the Catholic Cantons proposed sending an ultimatum to Zurich : it must either leave the Confederacy or reintroduce the Mass. But again no unity was reached among the opponents. Berne, Basle and Glarus had to bear in mind minorities which might soon become majorities. And so, in the end, all that was demanded of Zurich was that the orthodox Catholics should be allowed to celebrate one Mass a day in at least one church in the town. But, even against this, they remained steadfast and would not give way a hair's breadth. That was exactly Zwingli's way of working : he would wait long enough before he dared take action, but when he had once won something after hard fighting he would never bargain over it again. And it was this same unflinching stalwart attitude that made an impression on the Bernese ; from that time on, they gave up reprimanding Zurich. But the latter now entered into negotiations with Constance and Strasbourg.

Thereupon, the country cantons set to work in earnest and now, for the first time, used the anti-Lutheran movement in Germany to combat the Zwingli Reformation in Switzerland ; that is the meaning behind the Religious Conference in Baden, which began on the 21st May, 1526 and lasted for four weeks. Zwingli did not attend, by agreement with the Zurich authorities, for it was obvious from the start that this Disputation was to be a tribunal

OEKOLAMPADIUS (1481–1531)
from the oil-painting by Hans Asper

and not a debate ; and the memory of the death of the Stammheimer at Baden was still fresh enough in people's minds. And so Zwingli refused the invitation ; " I do not want to bathe at Baden ; the bathers (the people of Baden) steam and smell of sulphur." But, indirectly, his voice was heard there : a young man, disguised as a poultry-dealer, on several occasions brought letters from Zwingli, written to Oekolampadius, into the town, past the strict guardsmen at the gates. But the Conference proceeded just as the orthodox Catholics had cunningly planned ; then they ascribed the victory to themselves and decided to forbid the spreading of Zwinglian ideas and prevent the sale of his books by a strict censorship. This, however, only stiffened the attitude of Zurich. When, at the end of July, the Confederal States were to be newly sworn in, there appeared in the Limmat town only the representatives from Berne, Basle and Glarus ; the Catholic Cantons did not attend. Thus Zurich was put more and more on the defensive and it is from this point of view that we must understand its next action, taken on Zwingli's advice. At Christmas, 1527 the alliance with Constance was concluded and thereby Zurich stepped with one foot, as it were, outside the Confederation. The Reformer now considered similar protective alliances also with other south-German towns. " For even if the Word of God cannot be upheld by the strength of men, yet does God often bestow help and protection on humanity by using men as instruments and vessels, and, if God has set up such an arrangement, then it is clear that He will make use of it for good."

Zwingli met with his greatest success in Berne when a Disputation was held in the Barfuesser Church from the 6th till the 26th January, 1528. An impressive parade of all the forces of the whole of Protestant Switzerland, including Italians and brothers from southern Germany, was presented there. The Reformer had ridden with the Mayor and forty clergymen from the Zurich area under military protection into the city, where he had been awaited expectantly and was received most warmly. " What greater fortune could befall us citizens of Berne than that we should hear the Lord preached by Zwingli ! " He stayed with relations, perhaps in the same house where he had lived as a Latin student. A good 450 visitors had come for the Religious Conference ; it was opened by the reading of the ten Conclusions, of which the first and most splendid states : " The Holy Christian Church, of which Christ alone is the Head, was born of the Word of God ; remain ye in it and do not listen to the voice of a stranger." The most detailed dispute was that between Zwingli and Pastor Burgauer from St. Gallen about the Lord's Supper ; Zwingli preached twice in Berne and it was on one of these occasions that, so the story goes, an orthodox priest was about to make preparations for the Mass when Zwingli mounted the pulpit. " All right, I will wait until he has finished up there ! " the priest thought, but he never completed his task. For when he heard the Reformer speak so forcefully, he allowed himself to be taught by the better man and called out after the preacher's Amen : " if that is what the Mass is, then I will never celebrate it again, to-day or any day ". And he threw his vestment on to the altar; there it was to stay.

And the general results were most profound : all Catholic worship was now abolished in Berne, and here, too, Church administration was taken over by the Council ; soon there followed also the prohibition of foreign war-service and pensions.

Negotiations of a political nature were also carried on in Berne ; in consequence, this powerful Canton joined the Alliance on the 31st January. Zwingli's plans grew ever more ambitious : not only did he draw St. Gallen, Biel, and Muelhausen also into the Alliance but he now took up more and more the idea of a policy of conquest. He aimed at the destruction of the Catholic majority in the Federal Assembly, the abolition of the mastery of the old cantons over the ordinary bailiwicks (which in practice were already under the command of Zurich and Berne), the prohibition of pensions all over Switzerland and the toleration of the Protestant faith throughout the whole territory of the Confederation—in fact a complete and powerful reorganization in favour of the unhindered proclamation of the Word of God.

Feelings on both sides became more and more intense. Zurich declared that, where in the common domains there was a majority for the Protestant Faith, it would support this majority. This was most evident in the territory of the Abbot of St. Gallen and Thurgau ; in this way, Zwingli planned to extend the sphere of influence of Zurich to the Lake of Constance. And now, on the other side, the five Catholic Cantons thought they were justified in

79

taking measures for their own defence : on April 22, 1529, they made a solemn alliance with Austria. Then there came a conflict with Unterwalden, which demanded that Zurich should be expelled from the Federal Assembly for ten years, and that the Protestant pastor, Kaiser, who had been captured by the Schwyzer in Gasterland, should be executed. On the 8th July, Zurich declared war. " Peace is war and war is Peace "—this was pronounced zealously and resolutely by the same Zwingli who, previously, had condemned all warfare. For the sake of the Faith, he now considered it permissible and right to draw the sword ; naturally, he expected " that it would be waged without bloodshed, to the honour of God and the honourable town of Zurich," if they now suppressed with an overpowering demonstration the resistance of the enemy; before long, there was an army of 30,000 on the side of the Protestants against only about 9,000 Catholics, who were left in the lurch by Austria.

In spite of the Council's advice to the contrary, Zwingli joined in the campaign, with a halberd on his shoulder. But, at the moment when the Zurichers were about to cross the enemy frontier at Vorhut near Kappel, the bailiff of Glarus, Hans Aebli, appeared, bringing word that he had entered into peace negotiations and that, for the sake of God and the Fatherland, they must wait for the outcome. To Zwingli's disgust, this request found a hearing ; everyone wrote home to ask for instructions. Zwingli himself—these letters from the field have been preserved—appealed to the Mayor and Council of Zurich and warned them solemnly against making too hasty a peace. " Remain on your guard now and do not let yourselves be fooled by sweet words. Be brave for the sake of God ! Stand fast by God ! Do not give way to distress, until the right has been upheld."

Meanwhile, the many troops on both sides remained in the positions they had reached on the 10th June ; for a fortnight no one budged. Only the outposts of the Zurichers and Confederates met here and there. And, as they had been forbidden to harbour malice against each other, they became friendly and discussed bread, which the Five Cantons were unable to obtain, and milk, which the Zurichers lacked. On one occasion, some high-spirited fellows from the Five Cantons pulled along a tub of milk and put it on the frontier, so that it was partly on Zug territory and partly on Zurich territory. " We could, indeed, have some good milk," they called across to their opponents, " but there is no bread to break into it ! " The Zurichers appreciated the joke and also the hardship ; they set to and produced what was wanted from the bread bag ; and there the men of both sides lay spooning the milk and fishing out the scraps of bread. And if one of them stretched out his arm to catch something from the other half, he got his knuckles rapped from the other side : " You eat on your own ground ! " The mayor, Jakob Sturm from Strasbourg, who was in the Zurich camp all the time, was pleased about this and praised them : " You Confederates are indeed strange folk : even when you are quarrelling you are still united and do not forget your old friendship." And, in fact, Peace was made on the

24th June before a shot was fired. But Zwingli—he already knew the Glarus peace-maker, and had once been godfather to one of his boys—could not bring himself to thank him for his apparent kindness. With prophetic insight, he spoke to him : " Father bailiff, you will have to answer for this one day, before God. Be sure of this : as long as the enemies are in our clutches and unarmed, they will speak fine words, but afterwards, when they are armed, they will not spare us and then no one will make peace." And that is exactly what happened later on.

This was the first war in which the Puritan spirit went campaigning, in the persons of the soldiers of the Reformation. On the Zurich side, the strictest discipline and order reigned. Every day the men were marched with drums to the Service. Not a prostitute was seen, not a lascivious word was heard. Instead of dice and card-games, the troops amused themselves with jumping, throwing and putting the weight. They were even forbidden to touch the crops of either friend or foe. It was not surprising that everyone uttered a sigh of relief when the armies were able to turn back on their homeward way. Only Zwingli rode back over the Albis dissatisfied and with spirits dampened. He could see that this would not be the last conflict. And he knew why, henceforth, he must look more zealously for new allies. In the camp at Kappel, he had written and set to music the song that was afterwards sung, far and wide, even in the courts of princes :

Lord, Thou Thyself our course shouldst steer !
  That we may not go astray.
That will spoil the devil's play,
  Who Thee so wantonly doth scorn.

God, do Thou exalt Thy name
  And Satan punish, as before.
Awaken Thou Thy sheep once more,
  Who in their hearts do love thee well.

Grant that all our bitterness
  May perish with our feud.
Our faith must be renewed,
  That we may sing Thy praise for aye.

7

Nothing is more precious than love. Who would dispute that marriage is something most sacred ?

IT was not Zwingli's nature to tell us much about his family life ; about these matters he made far less display than others. But what he does by chance betray about them shows us the picture of a son, brother and husband who was deeply united with his own family and who looked after them faithfully.

All his life he was blessed by the influence of the large household from which he had sprung, up there in the Toggenburg mountains. His parents probably died when he was in Glarus. With his seven brothers and about three or four sisters, he maintained relations as best he could and for as long as it was possible. The two most promising of them he took under his own care and, with the sternness and kindness of a father, prepared them for study : the second youngest, Jakob, who at the time was already a young monk, in Glarus, and the youngest, Andreas, in Zurich. The first he sent, in the autumn of 1512, together with his favourite Glarus pupil, to Vienna ; in the letter of introduction to Vadian, Zwingli wrote that this brother of his had more than average ability and begged, humorously and yet seriously : " Clean, trim and polish him up with planes, axes and trowels. You will find him willing to do anything, I know. If he should dare to refuse, then hand him over, without any hesitation, to the prison, until his anger has cooled off. For the two years he will not get more than fifty florins and will, therefore, probably have to go sparingly." Quite suddenly Jakob died of the plague in 1517 and was buried in the Benedictine Monastery at Vienna, where he had probably been living. In deep sorrow Huldrych wrote to Vadian afterwards about the debts he might have incurred, saying he would pay them. Andreas, too, he lost at a most promising age ; he had been living with Zwingli and studying in Zurich since the spring of 1519, but he also fell a victim to the plague in 1520. Zwingli confesses he had " at first wailed and mourned madly like a woman ; for Andreas was a young man with great gifts and showed great promise. But, alas, the plague, which seems indeed to be envious of my blood and my fame, carried him off on Elizabeth Day ! "

Of his sisters, one of them probably kept house for him in Glarus, as later on we find that she had married there ; two others appear to have taken the veil in a convent near Wattwil, but later on, presumably on the advice of their brother, they gave up convent life and married. The other five brothers remained at home as miners ; a couple of them allowed themselves to be enticed into mercenary service, whereupon Huldrych wrote, in 1522, reprimanding them : " When I hear that you are living by the work of your hands, as behoves your origin, then I am happy, knowing that you are living up to the noble traditions of your ancestors.

But when I hear that you are entering into foreign wars, I am sad because you are abandoning the worthy state of peasants and workers."

From time to time his family thought they ought to warn this brother, who was becoming famous, about his headstrong beginning, and call him to order : he ought to proceed "with moderation". Similarly, a clerical relation, the Abbot of Fischingen, who loved Huldrych like his own child, once advised him that he ought to " go steady ". On the other hand, however, there were occasions when his relatives defended him bravely. For instance, once when they were sitting down with strangers for a drink in an inn, probably in Wattwil, two men of Schwyz began to jeer : " Master Zwingli is a thief and a heretic." This was heard by Joerg Bruggmann, Zwingli's mother's brother, who jumped up and dashed across the room with " the whole table after him "; there was a sharp clash and, in a violent fury, the uncle protested : " Master Zwingli is an honest man ! " And that was the end of it. Again, in 1531, when Zwingli appeared at the Synod in Lichtenstieg, Bullinger tells us that " Zwingli was held as dear and worthy as in his own country." And the last letter we have of Zwingli's is a petition to Vadian : Would he help his sick cousin, with whom he had lived from his childhood, to get into the St. Gallen hospital ? Another relative jokes, also in the last year of Zwingli's life : saying his attachment to his own home was so great that he could never pass a little dog that smelt of the Toggenburg without hailing it as a friend.

During the period before he was married, Zwingli

was looked after by a houskeeper named Margaret
an honest soul. In the house which at that time
served as his parsonage, the so-called *Leutpriesterei*
(secular priest's house) in the Cathedral Square,
where he lived from 1519 to 1522, there also lived, for
short or long periods, some of Zwingli's private
pupils from Glarus, Uri and the Toggenburg. There
was even a little boy, only eight years old, amongst
them. Zwingli's two assistants, Georg Staehli and
Heinrich Lueti, also belonged to the household ;
and it is possible there was also a little servant-boy,
whose duty it was to look after the horse and stable,
which the secular priest had at his disposal for his
extensive parish. The standard of living was
probably simple enough ; " I have a house, which
might content a Spartan in an emergency ", jokes
Zwingli himself, whose stipend was so small " that
it would scarcely sustain a miser or a poor peasant ".
Moreover, he was no financial genius : " My means
are scanty and I am no good at making ends meet."
But it was a happy household, full of hospitality and
cheerfulness. When the little Greek circle of younger
friends and Zwingli's own contemporaries met here,
what high spirits within those simple walls ! Or
when a young student was leaving, they knew how
to celebrate the occasion ; the maid would place a
garland of flowers on his head, to bid him farewell.
What excitement reigned after a festive evening !
For Zwingli was master of almost every instrument
of that time : the lute, the harp, the violin, the
Raboegli (pocket violin), the cornet, the French horn.
But he pursued these arts " with modesty ", as a
good friend reports ; it was more than foolish if

anyone interpreted it unkindly. Then he was liable
to get really angry ; " what impudent and ill-bred
asses they are ! After all, I have only been doing it
for the sake of a little domestic pleasure."

In the spring of 1522, Zwingli married a widow, the
same age as himself. Her maiden name was Anna
Reinhart and she was the daughter of the landlord
of the Little Horse Inn, Oswald Reinhart, and his
good wife Elsbeth Wynzuern, " an extremely
beautiful woman "; she was taken in marriage by a
noble Zuricher, the Junker Hans Meyer von Knonau,
against the will and behind the back of his parents,
who had probably wished for their only son, who
was always rather easy-going, a marriage more in
keeping with his station. They disinherited him ;
he was forced to enter foreign service and, as a
rifleman cadet in Italy, he caught the germ of an
incurable disease, of which he died in 1517. The
young woman, with her two daughters Margaret
and Agatha and her son Gerold, was left in a sorry
plight. The grandparents did, indeed, pay for the
children's education ; but they never fully accepted
her and, through her attorney, she had to carry on
unpleasant negotiations to obtain an annuity. The
" little court " in the Cathedral lane where she
spent her widowhood was not far from the
parsonage ; and so Zwingli probably soon noticed
her. And, in the Latin School of the college, he got
to know her son Gerold as well ; as early as 1521, the
latter wrote a short, intimate letter from Basle to his
Zurich teacher. No word tells us when Frau Meyer
of Knonau was first attracted to the secular priest
or why he wanted to marry her. One thing only is

certain—that in neither case were economic considerations decisive ; Zwingli defended himself
vehemently when people said he had wanted a rich
wife ! She had eventually—with enough difficulty—
secured from her noble relatives just about as much
as she needed to support herself and her children ;
and, for her part, she too found no improvement in
material conditions when she married her dear
husband. No longer did she wear her jewellery ;
she left her silk clothes lying in the chest and went
about " like any other ordinary working-class
woman ", to use Zwingli's own words.

Unfortunately, he kept his marriage secret for
two years, but one thing and another naturally
leaked out, which understandably gave rise to
gossip. It was certainly not fear for his own person,
but rather in order to spare his wife, who was still
carrying on the law-suit against her parents-in-law
and, above all, consideration for his own Cause, which
was by no means assured as yet, that made him
wait so long before announcing the marriage. At
last, when the fact that they were living together as
man and wife could no longer be concealed, " on the
second day of April 1524 did M. Ulrych Zwingli
wed Frau Anna Reinhartin, widow : and many
honest men were there to witness it." Meanwhile,
Zwingli had been obliged to change his official
residence and, after New Year 1523, he moved to the
corner-house " Zur Sul " in Church Street ; it was
here, then, that the Reformer began to taste the
joys and troubles of married life. And here his first
child was born, a girl, called Regula. He was still
in this house when she began to toddle ; and then

he had to move again a few houses higher up to the " Schoolhouse ", because he had now become Master of the college. And there he stayed for the short remaining span of his life, not quite seven years more ; and it was in this house that his wife presented him with three more children. After the birth of each one, the happy father made a note of the event at the back of his family Bible, never forgetting to name the god-parents. And by this means, too, we learn the reason for the choice of the name, in each case : all his boys and girls are called after their godmothers or godfathers. The entries, translated from the Latin, read : " Regula Zwingli was born in the year of our Lord 1524, on the last day of July, a Sunday, before daybreak, almost exactly midway between two and three o'clock. At her christening, she was carried by the curator, Heinrich Utinger and by the widow Regula Schwend, formerly the wife of Kaspar Murer of Basle. She was born in Zurich in the so-called Gandenheimer House, in the street leading to the new part of the town.—Wilhelm Zwingli entered the world in the year 1526 on the 29th January, at about eleven o'clock at night. At his christening, he was carried by Wilhelm von Zell and Anna Keller, the Prioress of the Oetenbach Convent. He was born in the so-called Schoolhouse.—Huldrych Zwingli, son to me, Huldrych Zwingli, was born in the year 1528, on the 6th January about midway between two and three in the morning. He was carried at his christening by Huldrych Trinckler and Elisabeth Lybin, the wife of the one-time mayor, Johann Effinger. He was born in the School-house.—Anna Zwingli was born to me by Anna Reinhart, who was also the mother of all the others above-mentioned, in the year 1530, on the 4th May, at ten o'clock in the evening. She was carried at her christening by the Provost Felix Frei of the Cathedral College and by the widow Anna von Griessenberg. She was born in the School-house."

Apart from this, we do not hear much about Zwingli's family life. But if it is a fact that the best marriages are those of which one hears least, this may certainly have been the case with Zwingli's. Now and again his wife was greeted by her husband's friends in letters. On one occasion she received some linen as a Christmas present from the monks of St. Gallen—it was in recognition of one of Zwingli's printed works dedicated to them. Shortly afterwards, he told his friend Vadian that the parson of St. Peter's, Leo Jud, had had twins, " whereby the world may see that the Almighty has given His blessing to the marriage of us clergymen." One single short letter of Zwingli's betrays the depth of his love for his wife. When he was staying in Berne for the Disputation, the news arrived of the birth of a little son ; whereupon he wrote the following brief note " to his dear housewife ": " Grace and peace from God ! Dearest wife, I thank God that He has bestowed on you a happy birth. May He help us to bring up the children according to His will . . . Herewith I commend you to God ! Pray for me and for all of us. Give my love to all your children, especially Margaret ; comfort her on my behalf. Huldrych Zwingli, your husband. Send me the Tolggenrock (dirty old overcoat) as soon as you can."

If we understand correctly, the step-daughter's trouble was that she had lost her first child ; she had been married the previous year to Anton Wirr.

Her sister Agathe was also married early, and her brother Gerold, when he was only seventeen. Zwingli seems to have been particularly concerned about the latter. This fact we owe to one of the Reformer's own important pedagogical publications. For when the boy, barely fourteen years old, returned from Baden, where he had been accompanying a relative who had been taking the waters, his step-father dedicated to him, as a " Baden present ", the little book that had been written for him and committed to print : " How to educate and teach young people in good morals and Christian discipline." And a warning is given there, amongst many other things : " Too much wine should be shunned like poison by a young man . . . It seems to me there is nothing more foolish than to seek honour and praise by wearing expensive clothes . . . When a young man first falls in love and favours someone, then shall he show what a chivalrous and strong nature he has ; he must guard against foolish love-affairs and choose someone to love, whose ways he will be able to endure for ever, even in marriage . . . He is not a Christian who only talks a lot about God, but he who makes an effort to do great things with the help of God. Consider nothing as hall-marks of distinction save virtue, piety and honour. Nobility, beauty and riches are not the true blessings of life, for they are subject to changes of fortune. May God lead you safely through these things, so that you may never be separated from

Him. Amen." We must add also that Zwingli the father, harassed as he was, always found time to be merry in the living room with his own family, to take down the lute from the wall and play something for the young folk or sing with them. He even once sent off the unappreciative, criticizing Chief Vicar of Constance with the droll remark that it was fortunate he was able to play : " it comes in useful for keeping the children quiet."

October 11, 1531 was a terrible day for Frau Zwingli. On that day, full of forebodings, she had to take leave of her Huldrych, who was going into battle. The next morning, she received blow after blow, the Job's messages of the death of her husband, her son Gerold, her brother Bernhard, a brother-in-law and a son-in-law ; they had all fallen in battle, in the marshland near Kappel ; and at home the children, the seven-year old little Regula and the five and three year old boys, waited in vain for their dear father's return ! Little Annie had already died while her father was alive. The twice-widowed mother and the little orphans found lodging afterwards with Zwingli's successor, Henry Bullinger, and she is said to have lived on for seven years after the death of her husband. Regula at the age of nineteen married Rudolf Gwalther, adopted son of Bullinger and later his successor in the office of chief district clergyman. Wilhelm went to the Latin School at Berne, afterwards to Strasbourg, where, as a young student, he died of the plague. The younger son, Huldrych, later became preachers' chaplain and Professor of Hebrew ; his first marriage was to one of Bullinger's daughters. The male issue of the

93

Reformer died out about a hundred years after his death, but there are still numerous descendants of our Zwingli living to-day under other names, throughout the town and land.

An attempt was made by a later writer to put into song the feelings of Anna Reinhart in mourning for her husband, of which we include here the first and last verses :

> O Lord, my God, how hard indeed
> Did Thy dire anger smite me !
> O my poor heart, canst thou still bleed?
> Is't not enough to fright me ?
> I wring my hands : could I but die,
> By grief and woe o'ertaken !
> Who knows my pain ? My God, my God,
> Hast Thou me quite forsaken ?

> Come thou, O Book, which met his needs !
> His comfort in all trouble.
> Whene'er pursued in words and deeds,
> Then turned he to the Bible,
> And there found help. Lord I would so
> From it such comfort seek.
> Give heart and strength in this great woe
> To me, so poor and weak.

8

The man who works resembles God more than anything else in the world.

WE have only a rough idea of Zwingli's outward appearance. It is still not known for certain whether, during his life-time, it occurred to a painter or an etcher to portray his likeness. It is possible that no less a person than the world-famous Albrecht Dürer painted him in the year 1516 ; this portrait, which has recently been given further consideration, does indeed show an exuberant personality. But the critics are still divided on the question as to whether it really represents the one-time pastor of Glarus. It is certain that the Zurich engraver, Jakob Stampfer, produced a medallion with the head of the Reformer, but this was probably done from memory after his death ; nearly all other pictures of Zwingli date back to this medallion which shows his profile, with his felt hat in bas-relief ; the oldest of these portraits is an oil painting by Hans Asper which is now in the Art Museum at Winterthur.

But we still have a few written descriptions by his contemporaries. The chronicler of St. Gallen, Johannes Kessler, says in his *Sabbatas* : " In appearance, he was a fine brave person of medium height, his face kindly and with a healthy colour." He always wore his dark scholar's gown and in this,

95

his everyday dress, he went into the pulpit. For travelling, he used to arm himself in the same way as everybody else ; an eyewitness of the Marburg Conference gives us a brief description : " He went about in a black tabard, carried a large bag and an ell-long weapon, called a Hessian, hanging down from his belt over the coat." His voice, as has already been mentioned, was not very strong ; Mykonius jokes about it somewhere : " People used to say that your voice was so soft that you could hardly be heard three paces away. But now I see that this is a lie ; you can, in fact, be heard throughout Switzerland. Obviously the Zurich wine has strengthened you so that now you preach with a stentorian voice." His eyes were not very sharp ; probably they suffered particularly from so much reading at night by the poor artificial lighting of those days. As early as 1525, we find him saying that, as far as he was concerned, one might just as well leave the " idols " hanging on the walls, " as I cannot see them properly, in any case ". Several months before his death he wrote in a letter : " Even I, with my bad sight, can see something worse than misfortune approaching."

And in other respects, too, he had from time to time to cope with ill-health ; on one occasion he tells us of the fever which prevented him from writing properly ; on another occasion we hear, as we have already noted, that he was staying in Pfaefers or Bad Urdorf for convalescence. When he was indisposed, he particularly liked to seek advice from his friend Joachim Vadian, in whom he had more confidence than in the Zurich doctors. In

April, 1526, he told Vadian : " To-day I found my-self in a difficult situation. I had preached early in the morning and, at 8 o'clock as usual, in the Prophecy School, had expounded a few passages from the Book of Exodus. Having gone for my bath at 9 o'clock and had myself bled, I nearly fainted on the way home. By the end of an hour I was more or less myself again, but only managed with difficulty to suppress the groaning which came from a weak heart, as my appearance betrayed. At two o'clock in the afternoon I was overcome by sleepiness—but as soon as I awoke, I was the old Zwingli again. I acted according to your former medical instruction ; you told me that, once a month, I ought to relieve my liverishness by taking preserve of roses." It seems, therefore, that from time to time Zwingli suffered hardship caused by liver or gallstones, upsets which sometimes broke out in acute attacks. But he had little time or inclination to look after himself !

He spent his time to the best advantage ; there was scarcely anything he did not manage to pack in-to his daily life. His biographer, Bullinger, tells us of this : " He used every hour sparingly and as industriously as possible, so that not a single one went by unused. He got up early in the morning." We have already seen how his morning was occupied. " After lunch he talked with his own good friends or received those who wanted to discuss any matter with him. From two o'clock until supper-time he read again. After the evening meal, he went out for a walk for a while and then read again or wrote letters, often until midnight." Thus, in addition to his many official duties as preacher, teacher and pastor, there were two things which took up a lot of his time : first reading, which to him seemed as indispensable as his daily bread (and there is no need to imagine that it was only the Bible and works of Christian exegesis which he read ; even in 1525 he wrote that he could not lend out his Greek Classics, for it was in them that he particularly liked to browse) ; and, secondly, his extensive correspondence, the radius of which extended far abroad. Moreover, he usually wrote really long letters. He would write one " with rumbling stomach ", another in intervals during the preparation of a sermon, and a third " after the sleeping-draught ". Kessler relates that Zwingli used to work in his study standing up, " leaning over a chair ", in an unheated room, dressed for cold weather, " so that, when he was studying, he was not overcome by sleep as he would have been if he were sitting down in a warm room ". Sometimes he used to write, as he himself confesses, " in the midst of so much work and with such a headache late at night that, if I did not see the pen running on, I would hardly know what was happening ". Moreover, it was sometimes so noisy round his house, " that before long I shall not know whether I'm on my head or my heels and whether I ought to move ". Sometimes it happened that he was interrupted ten times before he was able to finish a letter he had started. At other times the printers would worry him when he had a manuscript in hand. The smaller works he had to finish within a few days ; for longer ones, they started printing the beginning before he had written the end ; for this reason he was often unable to finish off his work properly, as he states with regret.

In short, he had so much to do, one way and another, that his colleague at the Fraumuenster Church said, on one occasion, that he only wondered that Zwingli hadn't gone mad by then. Even after he had gone to bed his brain worked on, until his thoughts became dreams. Once—it was during the night before Maundy Thursday, 1525, when he was to celebrate the first Communion with his congregation—the final clarification on the Protestant interpretation of the phrase " this is my Body " came to him in a dream, " through a messenger who came to stand beside me "—he woke up, jumped out of bed, opened the Bible and convinced himself of the correctness of what had just been secretly whispered to him ; and in the morning in the church he used the proof in the pulpit and thereby convinced some who were still wavering. Thomas Platter, who during the Baden Disputation helped as mediator in the aforementioned correspondence between Oekolampadius and Zwingli, tells of one of his journeys by night : " I was just in time to reach the gate (in Baden) and ran all the way to Zurich, went to the house of Mykonius, who was already in bed, and showed him the verdict. The latter said, ' Go then, and, even if Master Ulrich is already in bed, don't stop ringing until someone lets you in ! ' I rang so loudly that the sacristan living opposite got up and said, ' What a devil's life it is ! ' I said, ' Kaspar, I have come '. He recognized my voice and knew that I often came to see Master Ulrich. I rang again and, after quite a while, an old man named Gervasius came out, a former priest who had been living with Zwingli for several years. He told me to come in, saying, ' What do you want at this late hour ? Will you not let Master Zwingli have a night's rest ; he has not been to bed for six weeks ! ' And he knocked for quite a while on the door of his room. Zwingli came out at last, for he had heard that I was there, and rubbed his eyes. ' Well, you are a restless creature ; I haven't been to bed for six weeks and thought I would rest because it is Whitsun to-morrow.' In the room I told him what it was all about. Then he said, ' Zounds, is that all it is ? I must write a letter. Do you know a boy who could run back with it ? ' I said, ' Yes '. He said, If you would like something to eat, I will wake the maid, she will make you some soup.' I replied that I would rather go to sleep, wished him goodnight and sent him a boy. He gave him the letter and sent him off with it straight away."

Zwingli was equally untiring in serving and assisting people. His was a friendly nature ; a contemporary chronicler witnesses to this : " Moreover, he ate and drank with anyone who invited him ; he despised no one. He was merciful towards the poor." And the little events of daily life show us more of him as a man ; for example, when he presents a friend in Basle with a little cap from the Zurich Fair, or when he sends his dear friend Oswald Mykonius some whey from Glarus to Lucerne, and also when he receives from a follower in Zug, Roeteli, the present of a fish speciality from the Lake of Zug and thanks him for it in these words : " You have delighted my palate and overjoyed my heart."

4 66 35

Often he helped out with money, although he had so little to spare himself, " and as he paid nobody meanly for their services and was more inclined to be too good and generous than hard and sparing, he was often deceived by all kinds of dissemblers and brought to ruin where temporal goods were concerned." He put nothing aside for himself ; none of his writings brought him in any honorarium in hard cash : but, even though his income was small he never asked for any more. When he was offered something as a recognition of special efforts he had made, which were more of a political nature, he refused proudly : " My masters have provided me with sufficient nourishment and I need no recompense " ; and, on another occasion, he maintained, " I serve Christ and His Church, not my stomach. I have never wanted to take anything from any man ; so do not discredit the Grace of the Lord Jesus Christ ! " The house of this unselfish man became a shelter for people from far and near : " he received everyone kindly ; those who were exiled for their faith fled to him as to their father." The best example of this was the occasion when the German Knight, Ulrich Hutten, arrived in Switzerland, sick and penniless, and found the doors shut in his face at Basle. Zwingli immediately took in the brave warrior, sent him first to the spa at Pfaefers and then helped him to find refuge on the Island of Ufenau, although he, Zwingli, thereby completely forfeited the goodwill of the great Erasmus. And when Hutten died in his refuge, the Reformer still kept faith with him beyond death, and wrote to one of his creditors, " He has left simply nothing of any value.

He possessed no books and no household equipment beyond a pen. He owes me three florins, too—if I get anything back, I will accept it ; if not, it shall be a present. " Conrad Ferdinand Meyer recalls this fact : " Forget not, Germany, who it was who offered the last sanctuary and the last food to your Hutten."

But Zwingli took the same trouble over lesser people and treated them with equal kindness. Hungry children, whom he " fed daily " in Einsiedeln ; a poor seamstress, who could hardly carry on any longer ; a nun in the Fraumuenster who wanted information concerning a suitor ; a friend's mother, whose rich daughter-in-law did not treat her well ; to the latter he wrote, amongst other things : " Do not let your short life be disturbed by bitterness and unrest but make peace with each other " ; and warned them aptly, " Act in such a way that men may see how much better Christians are than the unbelievers ! " And Zwingli certainly had the right to call upon people to live peaceably together ; he got on so well with all his colleagues that there was never any ill-feeling. It is a good thing when a pastor can say, as he could, " I have always had reliable friends." To colleagues from Basle, who were not quite in agreement with each other, he wrote on one occasion, " Between us there is no secret resentment, no envy, no wrangling, no quarrelling." Zwingli was indeed, as far as is humanly possible, free from personal sensitiveness : " I am not, thank God, of such a tender nature that I am immediately wounded by every blow "—otherwise he would have stopped, before piling up so much enmity. He was capable of anger all right ; Bullinger tells us about his quick temper ; " but he never harboured ill-will for long ", and Zwingli himself confesses : " I am quick-tempered and violent ; but although I appear malicious and brutal, yet will I always belie this reputation." His, indeed, was the way of the truly great : in personal matters, easy-going and generous, for " what does it matter what becomes of me ! " but in the Cause, inexorable and ruthless in the extreme !

Even his humour testifies to his true sincerity— that humour which he had partly inherited from his parents and which was partly a result of his early environment in the Toggenburg ; not only the inhabitants of the neighbouring Appenzellen, but also those of the Thur valley, have always been known to this very day for their native wit. We have already heard how he was able to make his hearers laugh occasionally from the pulpit. For example, in his Lenten sermon, when he is confronting his opponents with the words of St. Paul : " If any of them that believe not bid you to a feast, and ye be disposed to go ; whatsoever is set before you, eat, asking no question for conscience sake " ; he hesitates a moment and adds, in parenthesis, smiling broadly : " But naturally this must be understood correctly, this 'whatsoever' does not, of course, mean everything, for he would be a frightful glutton who ate everything ! " But in his writings, too, he makes good use of funny anecdotes and humorous phrases. When he wants to censure an instance of thoughtlessness on the part of Luther, he says he was acting " just like that pastor who, having severely repri-

manded his flock, had concluded : ' See, if you do
not mend your ways and I mine then we shall both
go to the devil, and may God the Father, Son and
Holy Ghost help us in this! ' " Or he rails against the
offence of turning the Word of God into the words of
men, in order to attack it more fiercely : " It is like
a man who, not being allowed to beat his wife, takes
her by the apron, throws her down the stairs and
then excuses himself by saying that he had thrown
the apron downstairs." Or against the false doctrine
of the redemption of the sinner by the sinner :
" Like someone who is very ill hawking round
medicine which is supposed to be good for the disease
and teaching others how to use it, although he
cannot cure himself with it." And, laughing at weak
Christianity, which will not get down to work, he
remarks : " We are Christians just as much as
Doctor Starrenwadel (*i.e.*, with cramp in the leg) is
a rower and a sailor." Addressing those who did not
know their Bible, " You have flown from the nest
too early and your spirit has not yet assimilated
sufficient nourishment." The activities of the heretics must be stopped, otherwise " the crafty fellows
will multiply daily ". In the margin of an Augustine
commentary on the Biblical narrative of the Fall,
Zwingli notes down the joke : " O God, what a pity
that Adam didn't eat pears "—as though to say :
if he had preferred pears to apples, he would not
have experienced misfortune ! In the middle of a
serious exegetical treatise, the Reformer serves up
the amusing story : " A peasant was ill ; the doctor
prescribed him some medicine which he purchased
from the chemist. On the way home he regretted

having parted with so much good money. He hurried back and tried to reverse the bargain. The chemist replied, ' Certainly, I will take back the medicine, but I am not giving any money back ! ' " Now one can understand that the chronicler can well say, " Does anyone make better jokes ? " And Zwingli has faith in his listeners and readers : " Nobody will reproach us for a cheerful joke in the right place," he says. " But let nobody misinterpret it : ' It is not done for the sake of joking ; it is a serious matter ! ' "

Friend and foe alike must, however, allow our Zwingli one virtue : he was a brave man. One may rightly assert that for ten years Zwingli reckoned with growing certainty on the fact that he would have to die for his Cause ; again and again this suspicion is evidenced in his books and letters. In a letter as early as 1522, for example : " And so it must be ; the Christian faith was first firmly assured by the blood of Christ and then grew in glory through the suffering and bloodshed of its confessors. And so it must be purified again by much bloodshed." Already, two or three years previously, the idea had come across his mind as he was recovering from the plague, " Although sometime I must suffer the penance of death, perhaps indeed with greater torment than that through which I have just passed, O Lord." And, moreover, how often did his fate come very near to him before it finally laid hold of him at Kappel ! Once someone tried to murder him by night in a dark street ; someone tried to lure him from his house late at night under the false pretext of a request to visit a parishioner who was seriously ill. Another time three accomplices waited with pikes and horses, " their feet shod with felt ", outside the door of a house which they knew Zwingli was visiting ; they intended to give him " a knock-out blow " when he came out of the house and, by taking him away, to earn the 500 crowns that had been put on his head. On another occasion, when Zwingli and his friends were going to Berne for the Disputation, a shot, which was assuredly meant for the Reformer, was fired from the cover of a small wood just outside Mellingen. One night some Zurichers who were merry with wine, a weaver and a butcher, stood outside his house, banged on the front door and bawled, " Come out, red Uli ! That God's earth may put you to shame, you heretic, thief, seducer of the world ! Where is your little band of followers ? The same will happen to you as happened to the Baptists ! " Everything in disguised voices, so that they could not be recognized. And they smashed in the windows with paving-stones. Zwingli, who was anxious not to wake any of his family, got out of bed and with a weapon in his hand, looked to see if anyone had got into the house. Then, in a hushed voice, he called out, " What do you want with me ? Why don't you come for me by day ? " Thereupon one of the drunkards replied : " I thought you knew no fear." Zwingli : " I would not be afraid of you, even if I were with you in a dark wood." The drunkard : " Come down then ! " Zwingli : " I would come if you were a man of honour." And they sauntered off, cursing.

It was his firm faith in God which kept Zwingli

quite unafraid in the midst of all the dangers. " Without my confidence in the protection of the Lord ", he himself asserts, " I would long ago have given up the helm. But as I see that it is He who makes tight the ropes, sets the sails and even commands the waves, then I should not deserve to be called a man, if I left my post." And probably he had to struggle again for this certainty ; once he says in a letter to a friend : " Often do I pray and beseech the Lord greatly, in all the troubles and turmoils, which now beset the world and our town in particular, that the plague or any other disease may have mercy on me." And, again, a few months before his end, he actually lost his self-control and threw down the glove to the Zurich Council, saying that now he had had enough and was going to look for another place to work. And so it was not without reason that he often finished his letters with the request, " Let us pray for each other—by faithful prayer we will overcome everything." Zwingli himself prayed a great deal, as he told a close friend ; and he said that in this way he had grown stronger and felt more secure in the face of hardship. He once wrote, to encourage a pastor who was seriously ill, something which he had probably told himself more than once : " It was God's will that for a time you should administer the Word of His Gospel, but now He demands the proof in action. To talk in glowing terms of bravery when danger is far away, is weak and despicable ; but to be steadfast and undeterred when confronted with danger, that is the only sign of a brave heart." To what a wonderful breadth and depth did Zwingli's piety mature ! Apart from the circumstances of his death, this is best revealed by his two last writings : those on the subject of the *Providence of God* and the *Exposition of the Christian Faith*. The main point of them is: God is the only cause and power and the one goal of all that happens in the world ; everything is but the instrument of the divine Omnipotence and Wisdom. And Jesus Christ is the Captain and we are His " scions ", that is to say, His soldiers. " Thou art the tool of God ; He demands thy service, not thy resting ; how blessed art thou, that He allows thee to take part in His work ! " And He has His servants even among the heathen ; and the pious ones among them we shall meet in Heaven : " No righteous man has ever lived, no pious spirit, no faithful soul, from the beginning of the world unto its end, but will be found with God." And so Zwingli expressly confesses that, if he had the choice, then without any hesitation, he would prefer to share the lot of a Socrates or a Seneca than that of the Pope or one of the great ones of this world dependent on him.

9

I appeal to thee, O coming century. My view will certainly be victorious, victorious indeed.

AFTER the first few years of enthusiasm for Luther, Zwingli disavowed him decisively. Considerations of a tactical nature played their part in this at a time when the whole world was raging against the excommunicated Luther ; Zwingli did not want his Cause to suffer danger from the fact that people. might simply dismiss it as being the same as Luther's. " Dreadful is the anathema of Zeus (*i.e.*, of the Pope) ; therefore one must be on one's guard ", he writes, in the spring of 1521, to a trusted friend in Basle. From this it is to be understood that he defended himself when his opponents suggested he was tied to Luther's apron-strings : " I don't want the Papists to call me Lutheran ", he protested, in his interpretation of the Conclusions. And when he adds, " For I did not learn Christian doctrine from Luther but from the Word of God itself ", there is no need to charge him with distortion of facts. It is true that he owed to the amazingly bold Wittenberger definite personal encouragement for his own brave behaviour, but his perception of the Reformation came to him in other ways, independent of Luther. From the very beginning, therefore, in spite of the fact that, rather surprisingly,

109

they had many things in common, there became
apparent considerable differences in their interpretation of the newly-discovered Gospel. If one seeks
to throw some light on what, in the end, must
indeed remain the secret of their respective per-
sonalities, then one should consider the difference in
the outward and inward development of the two
men. Luther's early youth had been hard and his
later youth harder still ; Zwingli, on the other hand,
had been an enviable child of Fortune. Luther's
growth and development were characterized by
extraordinary struggles and an essential break with
the past, such as Zwingli never had to experience.
For Luther the question of salvation was and
remained the heart and soul of the conflict ; Zwingli,
on the other hand, started from the question of
truth, which did indeed lead him later to a realization
of the overwhelming significance of the question of
salvation. Luther was against all philosophy and
speculation ; these still appealed to Zwingli, even
after he had become convinced that the only certain
source of knowledge was the Biblical revelation.
For Luther, the most important thing was to find
objective guarantees that he had a merciful God :
Zwingli's endeavour was to find a conception of God
as pure as possible without any kind of human
additions. Using both terms in the best sense, one
might call Luther the Pietist and Zwingli the
Rationalist (*Aufklärer*) among the Reformers. This
was shown also in the different kind of outward
reforms : here Zwingli was the more radical, as a
result of his rational approach which enabled him to
grasp more acutely the pure teaching of Jesus, and

thus he perceived more clearly than Luther the un-christian nature of church form. Zwingli exhibited, in general, rather more of the optimistic, militant, nature of the Christ of the Synoptic Gospels : " All things are possible to him that believeth " ; whereas in Luther the pessimism of Paul is much more strongly apparent : " The world lieth in a state of wickedness." But, of course, one must not over-emphasize the secondary at the cost of the primary, in which they were both in complete agree-ment. For Zwingli, as for Luther, the centre of thought and faith and preaching was that Magna Carta of the Reformation : " The righteous man will live by his faith " ; but they do not give quite the same emphasis to this slogan ; Luther puts the emphasis more like this : " the righteous man will live by his *faith* ", whereas Zwingli stresses : " the righteous man will *live* by his faith." And just as the starting-point of their development as Reformers was different—in the case of Luther it was : " What must I do that *I* may be saved ? " and for Zwingli it was rather the question : " What can be done that my fatherland may not perish ? "—so Luther under-stood the Kingdom of God as something completely personal and invisible, in which no outward law and no state had the power or right to intrude; while for Zwingli, although the living faith concealed in the heart was, indeed, the first and most decisive factor, it must nevertheless show its genuineness also in the outward order of public affairs and be in a position " to restore the dominion of God on earth ", as he himself stipulates. According to Luther, the Christ-ian does not have to bother himself with politics ;

that is the job of the secular princes. Zwingli, as a Republican, not only taxed the authorities with their Christian responsibility, but also called upon all the people to play their part. The ethic of both Reformers was : " Do right and suffer wrong ! " but with Luther the emphasis lay more on the latter and with Zwingli more on the former. And that resulted for each of them in a greatness that was not achieved by the other : for Luther the heroism of patience, for Zwingli the heroism of action. Both of these have their dangers, if the one will not learn and be warned by the other. Lutheranism has to be careful not to fall into quietism and liturgism ; the Zwinglian Reformation, on the other hand, has to guard against degenerating into venality and legalization.

In view of the considerable points of friction, of which the doctrine of the Lord's Supper was only one, it was inevitable that these two prototypes should clash sooner or later. And that each of them should put all his might into the support of what, to his own way of thinking, appeared to be the Biblical Truth, was only right and indeed, to his own conscience, a sacred duty. Only it was unfortunate that the battle over both material objectives and fundamental principles was not always carried on with the personal noblesse which might have been expected of Christians of this standing. In the course of the long disputes it was rumoured that, to an increasing extent, the opponent was insisting on his own doubtful viewpoint out of sheer dogmatism and obstinacy. Especially did Luther regard the peculiar attitude of the Swiss as obstinate eccentricity, and attributed to Zwingli motives of ambitious lust for

dictatorship ; indeed, he even went so far as to
forget himself by declaring that his rival in Zurich
was carrying on his work possessed by the devil.
The accused was able to defend himself at length :
" How does it come about that the poor devil is held
responsible for everything ? I thought the devil
had already been overcome and received his sentence. If the devil is a powerful master of the world,
as you have said, how can it be that all things are
done according to the providence of God ? " But
Luther still stood by this disparagement, principally
because Zwingli did not condescend to consider any
other than his own conception of the Lord's Supper.

Probably they both had the same ideas on this
subject originally, that is to say, at the time when
they were both fighting, for the very same reasons,
the sacramentalism of the Roman Church, which was
in contradiction to the clear words of the Bible. But
then their ways parted ; Luther, on the one hand,
interpreting the words of the Institution of Baptism
and the Lord's Supper literally, merely divested
these two signs of the magical elements of the Catholic Church, but retained them nevertheless as sacra-
ments ; whilst Zwingli, on the other hand, proceeded
more consistently and more radically. Above all, as
regards the Lord's Supper he warned people against
investing it with mysteries, about which the Gospel
accounts tell us nothing. Bread and wine are not
means of salvation but only tokens of communion
and symbols of duty. Just as the people of Glarus
gather together each year on the anniversary of the
Battle of Nefels in memory of the fight of their
fathers, and thereby vow mutual faith to their

country and nation, so, in the Supper, Christians celebrate the memory of the redemptive death of the Lord, pledging themselves anew in His Cause. And, just as a bridegroom gives unto his beloved a golden ring, saying : " Take this, this is myself ", although the ring is not, of course, the bridegroom himself but merely represents him and will make the bride joyful in the certainty of the love and fidelity of her husband, so in the same way, are bread and wine an impressive indication, for the faithful, of the salvation that was won for us on the Cross and a sure token of the reconciliation that was made there.

The battle of the two conceptions, which had first been opened by skirmishes between followers of Luther and those of Zwingli, was waged for a long time. Later they themselves joined battle with their writings, sometimes in Latin, sometimes in German. With growing decision and violence, the Wittenberger emphasized the miracle which takes place in the Lord's Supper, in accordance with the words, which should be taken literally : " This is my Body—this is my Blood." And Zwingli never tires of quoting the other passage to contradict it : " It is the spirit that quickeneth ; the flesh profiteth nothing." He said it was clear that what Jesus meant by the words, " this is my Body ", was that it represented Him. Whereupon Luther replied that, in that case, one might as well explain the whole Bible away symbolically, translating the first sentence like this : " The cuckoo ate the hedge-sparrow." " Cuckoo " means " God ", " ate " means " created ", and " hedge-sparrow " means " heaven and earth." " You must keep to the Word ! " It is obvious how painful was this quarrelling among their own ranks and how it hindered the advancement of the common Cause. And so a Protestant prince, the young Landgrave, Philipp of Hesse, made an attempt at a reconciliation. In correspondence with Zwingli he grew to realize that, in order to promote an effective Protestant policy of alliance, it was now imperative to bring together the estranged brothers and to come to a united declaration on the most important doctrinal questions. He, therefore, invited both parties to a Disputation at his castle at Marburg, actually asking Luther without letting him know at first that Zwingli was coming as well ; otherwise, in his ill-humour, he would probably not have accepted. Our Reformer left Zurich secretly ; even his wife was not allowed to know where his journey was taking him. In Basle he was joined by Oekolampadius ; and Bucer and Hedio came from Strasbourg ; a band of municipal workers from Zurich and Basle formed their escort through the German territory, which was by no means without its dangers. The Swiss were the first to arrive and, when they entered Marburg in the early morning of September 27, 1529, they were received in the most friendly fashion by the Landgrave ; he had already sent out forty armed men to provide safe conduct for the expected guests. Soon the German counterpart arrived : with Luther were his most outstanding co-belligerents from Wittenberg, Melanchthon and Justus Jonas ; Osiander came from Nuremberg, Brenz from Swabia and Agricola from Augsburg. In addition, there came the Council's representatives and theologians from Hesse itself,

Ioannes Oecolampadius ƒſ

Huldrijchus Zwinglius

Martinus Bucerus

Caspar Hedio

Martinus Luther
Iustus Jonas.

Philippus Melanchthon

Andreas Osiander

Stephanus agricola

Joannes Brentius

under the leadership of the Professor there, Franz Lambert.

At six o'clock in the morning of October 2 there began the Disputation which was to last several days. The Landgrave's Chancellor greeted the visitors ; on the one hand Luther with his following, on the other hand Zwingli with his satellites ; and gave an impressive warning that they should not grant the common enemy the pleasure of seeing that there could be no peace made between the evangelical brethren. Luther took up a piece of chalk and wrote with firm strokes on the desk in front of him : " This is my Body." Oekolampadius was the first to speak and, quoting other passages from the Scriptures, such as " John is Elias ", or " the seed is the Word ", said, " Cannot then the expression ' This is my Body ' just as easily be interpreted symbolically ? " Luther replied : " What do you mean by ' cannot ' ? It is a matter of proving that it *must* be understood in this way." " That I will gladly prove ", said Oekolampadius and opened his New Testament at the sixth chapter of St. John's Gospel, where Jesus says " I am the Bread of Life " ; but when the disciples and Jews took it literally, he explained to them : " It is the spirit that quickeneth ; the flesh profiteth nothing." Is it not then as clear as day, said Oekolampadius, that Jesus would have nothing to do with the physical partaking of His Body ? Luther replied : " In this case certainly, but, in the case of the Last Supper, he was instituting a physical meal." And, pointing to what he had written in chalk, he said : " For this I have a powerful text; this should be sufficient ground for

men to believe that it is the Body of Christ."
Oekolampadius objected : " Is not one thus attach-
ing too much importance to material things ? " To
which Luther replied : " What do you mean by
important and unimportant ? It is not a question
of *what* is said but of *who* says it. If God commands
us to pick up a straw, then that is something most
important." Then Oekolampadius asked whether,
since, after all, we have spiritual food (meaning :
faith in Christ the Saviour), it is then necessary to
have physical food as well ? Luther became more
violent : " I am not asking whether or not it is
necessary ; I am a prisoner of the Word of Christ.
If Christ should command us to eat dirt (here Zwingli
shook his head : ' He does not command us to do
that ! ') then I would do it, knowing that it would
be for my good. A servant should not put his own
ideas above the will of his master. One must close
one's eyes." Oekolampadius asked : " Where is it
written that we should go through the Scriptures
with our eyes closed, Herr Doctor ? " Luther's reply
was that they might go on arguing for a hundred
years and never get anywhere. " Dispose of this
text for me and I will be satisfied," he said, putting
his finger on the desk again ; " if you cannot do so,
nor can I."

Then Zwingli joined in and began talking in quite
calm and friendly tones : " I am speaking the truth
when I say that I am very pleased to meet you face
to face, Doctor Luther, and you, Philip Melanchthon.
Let us forget the unkind words that have already
passed between us. But we, too, have a text to write
on the desk, namely this, that the flesh profiteth

nothing, and this passage undoubtedly follows on from the question of physical food. If, therefore, you are in agreement with us in that the Lord's Supper is a matter of faith, then I pray you for the love of Christ, not to abuse us as heretics ! Do not take this amiss ; I should like to have your friendship." Luther gave the assurance that he wanted to control his feelings but, nevertheless he insisted that the spiritual partaking does not exclude the physical. Granted that wherever the Word of God is proclaimed, there salvation is acquired through faith alone ; but, if God wishes us also to partake physically, then we must not oppose Him. " Then we partake in faith of the Body, which is given for us. The mouth receives the Body of Christ, the soul believes in His words while it partakes of His Body. Here stands the clear Word, ' This is My Body ' ; all you do is make criticisms ; you probably mean well, but that is not the point."

Zwingli mentioned numerous Biblical illustrations where " is " obviously means " represents ". In his opinion, one must extract the essence from the Word. The Supper is and remains a symbol ; it is to be delivered unto Christians so that they may thereby bear witness that Christ died for them. To which Luther replied : " I am not arguing about ' is ' and ' represents '. Christ says ' This *is* my Body ' ; that is sufficient for me and no devil can make me think differently. We must be obedient to the Word of God and not set ourselves above it. Therefore. glorify God and believe the pure words of the Scriptures." To which Zwingli replied : " We exhort you, too, to the same end, that *you* glorify

God and give up your preconceived opinion. We do not give up our text : ' The flesh profiteth nothing ', so easily either, and you, Herr Doctor, will have to strike a different note." Luther : " You are speaking in hatred." Zwingli : " Then declare at last whether you will let John 6 stand as it is ! " Luther replied : " Herr Zwingli, you are trying to overwork it." And Zwingli : " Well, well, it is just that passage that will break your neck." Then Luther became angry ; " Don't be too sure of yourself ! Our necks don't break as quickly as that. You are in Hesse now, not in Switzerland." Zwingli smoothed over the quarrel : " Are we then always to take everything literally ? at home we only talk like that when we know our cause is lost."

The next morning—it was Sunday—Zwingli preached first on the Providence of God ; then the debate continued about the omnipresence of the Body of Christ. " No ", the Swiss and the Strasbourgers tried to show, " the Body of the Lord can only be in one place ; now it is sitting at the right hand of God the Father and does not come down into the Bread of the Lord's Supper." But Luther would have no bargaining ; he pointed rigidly to the desk where it was written : " This is my Body ". " One cannot squeeze out that little phrase or give it another meaning. The Word, the Word, the Word, do you hear, is the decisive factor." Finally the Landgrave asks if they really cannot reach agreement ; to which Luther remarked : " The only way I can see to do that is that they (meaning the Swiss) glorify God and believe what we do." And, as his opponent was silent, Luther continued : " Then I

must let you depart, and commit you to the judg-
ment of God." At this remark, Zwingli's eyes grew
moist. Did the Wittenberger notice it ? Briefly,
Luther thanked his friend from Basle, for so kindly
leading his Cause ; he thanked the Zuricher and
asked his pardon if he had used too harsh words
against him. " I am, after all, only flesh and blood
and should indeed be glad if the dispute could be
settled." To which Zwingli replied that he too was
sorry for his violence ; he had always wanted to have
the friendship of Doctor Luther and still wanted it.
" I know no men in Italy or in France whom I would
rather have met than you men of Wittenberg." It
was unfortunate that, at this point, the Strasbourgers put their spoke in the wheel again, and
harassed Luther with the question, whether he now
recognized the correctness of their belief in every
point ? Luther protested : " In faith, no, I am not
your master and your judge ; I hear you now,
indeed, but do not know that this is your teaching
when you are at home. Our spirit and your spirit
do not agree, but rather it is obvious that we do not
have the same kind of spirit." Again the Landgrave
made one last attempt : he called one and the other
to him separately and pleaded earnestly : whether,
in spite of everything, they could not promise each
other help and loyalty in the common Cause ? Yes,
indeed, said Luther and his followers if Zwingli and
his satellites would acknowledge that the Body of
Christ is present not only in the memory of men, but
also in the Supper itself—if so, then they on their
part would not ask any more about the How and the
When. But when the Zuricher was asked for his

121

agreement, he would not, could not subscribe. He would not let it be said of him that he had deviated one hair's breadth from the straight path of truth for the sake of outward gain ; and Oekolampadius joined in this refusal.

And yet they did not want to part, with hands completely empty : in all haste a written statement was made of the points on which, for the sake of the Protestant faith, both sides were agreed. This Confession of the Marburg Articles was signed by the representatives of both parties, free of all mistrust and with the vow that, in future, they would cease violent writings against each other. The last sentence of the agreement reads thus : " Although we have not reached an agreement at this time on the question as to whether the actual Body and Blood of Christ are physically present in the Bread and Wine of the Lord's Supper, yet shall each side show Christian charity to the other, in so far as it is compatible with their conscience, and both sides shall pray devoutly to God the Almighty, that He, through His Spirit, will strengthen us in true understanding. Amen."

10

*We must so dedicate our senses, once and for all,
that we are inseparably bound to Right and Truth and
God, even at the cost of our possessions and life*

ZWINGLI brought back one prize from Marburg :
the friendship of the Landgrave of Hesse. From
now on they were truly bound together by an intimate correspondence ; in this, when discussing
particularly delicate matters, they made use of
coded names, to which no one else had the key. It
was a matter of risky political plans : a far-reaching
anti-Hapsburg alliance was to be formed, which
would unite in common action Saxony, the Rhine
towns, Württemberg, even Venice and France, as
well as the Protestant part of Switzerland. They had
even gone so far as to enter into negotiations with
Venice and France, although in fact these came to
nothing. Of all these great and all too risky projects,
the only one that was realized was the recognition
of the sovereign rights of Hesse. Another proposed
entente was rejected by Zwingli himself, namely
that with the Schmalkaldic League; it was repugnant
to him to acquiesce in an agreement that, in his eyes
was only a half-measure.

The advance of the Protestant Cause in the Confederation was now pressed more forcefully, following the " First Land Peace of Kappel ". The former

territory of the Abbot of St. Gallen remained under the occupation of Zurich troops ; Zurich even granted a constitution to the League of the Christian Cantons. Gasterland and Thurgau had virtually become, in fact if not in name, provinces of Zurich ; Zwingli was already presiding over the Synod at Frauenfeld. In the province of Glarus the celebration of the mass was forbidden ; in Solothurn, too, the victory of the Reformation seemed a certainty. And the way things were developing in Geneva and Neuchatel promised well. Zurich and Berne were well on the way to becoming joint masters of Switzerland ; but Zurich had the upper hand. And, in the Limmat town itself, Zwingli's power had by now become absolute, as it were. He was Zurich's Burgomaster, Town Clerk and Council all in one, as was admitted even by the Catholic historian of that time. The Bernese Reformer, Berchtold Haller, calls him " Bishop of the whole Fatherland and Eye of the Lord ", and another time " Guardian not only of the Fatherland, but of the whole Christian Community."

But now all of a sudden the terrible reversal began. As though all had been conspiring against him, one after another turned against Zwingli : all the open resistance from the enemy side and all the opposition in his own ranks, which hitherto had only been forced into silence. Naturally enough, the Catholic Cantons would not be satisfied with the way things had developed so unfavourably for them ; their bitterness about the transfer of power within Switzerland increased in the extreme and drove them again to an Austrian alliance. Zwingli heard about

BERCHTOLD HALLER (1492–1536)
from the wood-cut in Reusner's *Icones*

it and wanted to paralyse his opponents' desire for attack by a powerful, quick advance, as had been made two years previously. But Berne hesitated now and refused its support, and this was not merely because the Bernese sympathized with the Catholic Confederates, for they had been the first to suggest imposing an economic blockade on them. The main reason was the fear that Zurich might become too strong. Zwingli resisted the merciless, stupid half-sanctions of Berne saying, " He who abuses another as a liar to his face, must of necessity fight with word and fist together. For, if he does not strike, he will be struck. And so, if we refuse provisions to the Five Cantons, as being criminals, we ought now to follow up this action and not leave poor innocent people to starve. But, as long as we sit still as though we had not sufficient cause to strike, and neverthe-less deprive them of food and drink, we force them to punish and strike you ; and that will certainly come to pass." But the warning was of no avail ; in May, 1531, the blockade began. In June, Zwingli composed a memorandum with the bold programme : Berne and Zurich ought now to take on the leader-ship of the Confederation, " like two oxen in front of the cart, pulling with *one* yoke, so that hence-forth nothing more can be decided within the Con-federation without their consent."

But now events came rushing upon each other in a most disastrous manner. In Zurich itself, there were people who were in league with the Five Cantons and Austria ; once again the old aristo-cracy dared to resist more openly. The strictly-enforced moral mandates had damaged the popularity of the Reformer with a section of the citizens and peasants ; and now the millers, bakers and butchers were complaining about the damage their trade was suffering as a result of the food blockade. Moreover, people were tired of new levies for belligerent actions, and the economy measures that had just been taken with regard to the soldiers' pay were not calculated to strengthen a desire for military preparedness. Zwingli was losing more and more ground and also losing contact with the people ; and so, on the 26th July, he came before the Council and citizens with a request to be relieved of his post. He said he would look round for work elsewhere if they would not listen to his advice any longer. That, indeed, had the effect of a warning shot and they begged him earnestly and with the finest promises to stay whatever happened. But his position remained undermined, nevertheless.

His chief aim still was to remove the main obstacle ; the negative attitude of Berne. With this end in view, he went, on August 11, to the manse at Bremgarten to discuss matters with the friendly-disposed Councillors of Berne—this, too, in vain ! Before daybreak Zwingli left the house of his young friend, Henry Bullinger, which was guarded by three faithful men. It was Henry Bullinger, who, so soon afterwards, was to become his successor in the Cathedral pulpit. The latter accompanied him to the Zurich frontier where Zwingli, with tears in his eyes, took his farewell, saying : " My dear Henry, God preserve thee and be thou true to the Lord Christ and His Church ! " Zwingli was full of uneasy forebodings. The following incident is related.

One day he went with the Abbot George Muller of Wettingen to the cemetery of his dear church. There was a comet in the sky. And when his friend asked him what was the significance of that, Zwingli replied : " My dear George, it will cost my life and those of many men of honour, and the Truth and the Church will suffer much distress ; but Christ will not desert us."

In the first few days of October the Five Cantons drew up their army near Zug, news of which reached Zurich at first only by way of rumour and without any details. It was not till October 9 that it became obvious that the declaration of war might come at any hour. And so, towards noon of the following day, the Zurich advance guard marched out, led by George Goeldli who was anything but reliable ; his brother was in the opposing army, his family were among the supporters of mercenary warfare. In the afternoon the alarm was raised, first in the country and afterwards in the town ; there could be no question of the main army starting before the next morning. In Zurich, great confusion reigned. The troops, hurrying in from all sides, lacked the necessary order ; neither were there enough horses to draw the guns and baggage. And the muster of soldiers did not, by a long way, attain the numbers that were expected and absolutely essential ; only about 1,500 armed men, mainly, of course, the most fervent supporters of the new faith, finally entered the field behind the Zurich banner. The commander-in-chief was the bailiff of Kyburg, Rudolf Lavater, the standard-bearer was John Schwyzer, who, in spite of his seventy years, was still a vigorous man.

And Zwingli went with them. In accordance with ancient custom, the town pastor had to accompany the army ; who else could it be, in this case ? Before mid-day he became separated from his own followers. Equipped as a chaplain, with helmet, armour and a sword, he mounted the horse, carrying a little Bible in his shoulder-belt. It is said that at this moment his mount shied, which was regarded as a bad omen. As they were riding over the Albis, a man who was near him heard the Reformer praying half aloud. Yonder now was the advance guard, a mighty throng in front of Kappel. Goeldli had drawn them up in an unfavourable position : on their left was marshland, on the edge of which was an unguarded wood ; in the rear was a ditch with only a narrow little bridge.

When the main army reached the nearby village of Hausen, a short halt was made and it was debated whether they would not do better to wait for the much needed reinforcements ; at this Zwingli shook his head, saying : " If we stop here for long to collect ourselves, I fear we shall be too late for our honourable comrades. Therefore it is not right that we should look on while our men suffer down there. I for one will go down to them in the name of God and either die with them or help to rescue them." And so they pushed on. In the end the horses were left behind and the troops in the marshland grouped themselves in battle formation. Zwingli, like the other chaplains, joined one of the front ranks. A baker from Zurich who hitherto had not been known as specially zealous in the Reformation Cause, now called out across to the chaplain : " Master Ulrich,

how do you like it now ? Is this to your taste ?
Who is going to stomach this ? " To which Zwingli
replied, as though it were a matter of course, " I and
many honest men here who are still in God's hands,
be we alive or dead." But the other added—and
kept his word— : " I too will help you out and risk
life and limb in your support."

It was already nearly sunset when the attack was
launched from out of the beechwoods, behind which
the army of the Five Cantons had been taking cover.
With the battle-cry : " Heretics, vandals, soul-
murderers ! " they break forth : the Zurichers shout
back in reply : " Idolaters, crown-eaters, blood-
suckers ! " Schwyzer, the standard-bearer, urges :
" Now for it, my dear friends ! " Lavater, the
captain, gives the command : " Bear yourselves
like honest men ! " Already the combatants are
falling upon each other ; the first victims are sinking
into the marshy grass. Zwingli encourages his men.
raising his voice aloud : " Dear Zurichers, be
valiant ! It will mean toil and sweat but God will
be with you." And, indeed, it really seemed at the
second advance that victory was inclining to the
side of the Reformers. But soon the tide turns ; the
enemy, who are far superior numerically, throw
more and more troops into the battle. A frightful
hand-to-hand fight begins. The Zurichers are so
closely massed that they are no longer able to use
pikes and axes properly, which results in hopeless
confusion. In addition, a section of the army of the
Five Cantons has completed a movement to the left
and now falls on the Zurichers in the flank, takes
them by surprise and forces them back towards the

mill-race. A traitor from Zug, who gets among the Zurichers, shouts out : " Flee, you are lost, you won't get away with your lives ! " But they go on fighting resolutely. And the troops are mown down like corn at harvest-time.

And it is the end for Zwingli too. He will not budge from the spot and goes on, joining in the fighting, with those in the front. And he does not tire of exhorting the others to hold out : " Brave men, be comforted and be not afraid ! Commend yourselves to God ! He will look after us and ours." And then he is struck in the leg ; but he gets up again. Another blow on the thigh, so that the blood streams forth ; but he does not turn round. Then one of the enemy gives him a merciless blow on the helmet ; that lays him out on the ground and he cannot rise again. " They can kill the body but not the soul ! " he groans. And over him the warriors pound away.

Those who are still alive are driven back to the stream, where many of them find a watery grave. Some manage to cross the little bridge but are then pursued towards the Albis. Only the oncoming night brings an end to the cruel destruction. The wounded and dying wail, groan, pray, and from what they say one can tell to which side they belong : the Zurichers call on God and the Lord Christ, those from the Five Cantons, however, call on the Mother of God and the dear Saints. And there are plenty from the enemy ranks who have pity on the wounded Zurichers and would fain comfort them ; they say it is such a pity that so many good, honest fellow-Confederates should perish. Others scold violently, saying they got what they wanted ; if their faith were the right one, as they pretended, then God would have helped them, Friend and foe alike are asked whether a priest should be called, to whom they can make the last confession.

In the general confusion some of them come across Zwingli, without recognizing him at first. He is lying on his back, still alive, with his hands clasped as though in prayer, and looking up to the stars above. They ask him whether, as he is so weak and near to death, he would like a priest to be called, while there is still time. At this, Zwingli shakes his head and goes on looking up to the sky. Now they advise him : if he does not want to make a last confession, then he should inwardly call upon the Mother of God and the Saints, entreating them to plead for God's grace for him. Again Zwingli shakes his head and continues to stare up at the sky. In the end, the others say, " It must be one of those wicked heretics ; die then as you deserve ! " And a captain from Unterwalden draws his sword and gives him the death blow.

It is not till the next morning that anyone realizes who it is lying there in his own blood. And then there is a great stampede ; everyone wants to see him whom they accuse of being the most to blame for all the disaster. Then it is debated what is to be done with his corpse. Some of them want it to be hewn into five pieces and one of these symbols of victory to be sent to each of the Five Cantons ; others want the body to be burned, as befits a heretic. And although a few captains urge that the dead man should now be left in peace, revenge gains the upper hand with these irreconcilable zealots. But, before the news of the sad story is proclaimed in Lucerne, the priest from Zug, Hans Schoenbrunner, arrives ; he knew Zwingli from Zurich and had occasionally heard him preach. He now raises his hand as if to bless the defenceless man and, hardly able to restrain himself from weeping, speaks the words which form the funeral oration for him whom no grave will contain : " Whatever you may have been by reason of your faith, I know that you were an honest Confederate."

Zwingli was forty-seven years and nine months old when he died on the field of battle with 500 Zurichers, including 25 like-minded clergy. By human standards he died too early ; for his work was far from being completed, and never were his brave words and wise counsel more needed than at this very time, after the sad outcome of the second Kappel campaign and the further defeat that was suffered shortly afterwards at Gubel. That which the Reformers had feared came to pass : for, when in the middle of November the peace treaty was made, the Zurichers and their Protestant Allies lost much of the ground they had already gained. They were obliged to dissolve the bonds of citizenship with the Protestant towns and merely look on while, in the common domains, majority rule prevailed, without toleration for the Protestant minorities. Thus the free bailiwicks and the Gasterland became completely Catholic again and the Monastery of St. Gallen went back to the Abbot. Solothurn, too, was lost to the Reformation and in Appenzell and elsewhere the movement came to a standstill. And

most discouraging of all was the fact that in Zurich
itself the opposing party threatened to come to the
top again. Mykonius realized this, and that was why,
when he heard the news of Zwingli's death, he called
out : " God have mercy ! Now will I no longer
remain in Zurich." Even the more determined
Reformers thought for a while that all was now lost.
Zwingli's Cause must indeed have been a good one,
or it would undoubtedly have gone under at this
time. He had been right in his prophecy, made as
much as ten years before his death : " I am certain
that the Truth will conquer, even though my bones
may be burnt to ashes."

Indeed, one may well maintain that Zwingli
continued to work in an astonishing manner after
he had left the scene of action. It was the spirit of
Zwingli which made Bullinger, when only twenty-
seven, take over the helm in the midst of the storm
and remain there so bravely and sensibly for forty-
four years. It was the spirit of Zwingli which,
again and again, purifying and fructifying, swept
over town and country and from Zurich drove the
Confederacy to deeds of courage for the sake of the
Faith. It was the spirit of Zwingli which, through
hidden channels, also reached Geneva, whence,
through the medium of its great Reformer, John
Calvin, it resounded to a whole world of Protestant
peoples, wherever they might be. It is the spirit of
Zwingli which is still at work to-day in its homeland
and in many a distant land, even though its source
is now hardly recognized. And this legacy of Zwingli's, the effect of which is still being felt, has
certainly not escaped those paralysing influences to

which all great spirits are subjected by posterity—
misrepresentation, limitation and doctrinarianism.
Zwingli's spirit, too, was lost in the emphasis on the
letter of his teaching, his freedom was turned into
constraint, his living vitality into dead banality.
And, after his death, the Catholic element even crept
back into his evangelical Church. His Reformation
is still not complete ; never was that fact clearer
than in the failures of the present age. We must
carry on his work with renewed determination, with
greater boldness. Now, above all, we must understand and act upon that which was the very heart
and soul of Zwingli's message : that we need not be
dismayed by the so-called necessities of this world.
Nothing is necessary except that God's will be done.
Therefore he calls upon us to fight on, sword in hand.
And he points to the Bible which he carries under
his arm, saying : This is the best weapon, the only
one that will be victorious, the Word of God !
" May God send His thunder and hail upon us if we
allow the Holy Scriptures to be distorted. Take care
that the divine Word is loyally proclaimed amongst
you ; thereby you will preserve your Fatherland,
even though the devil oppose it. Listen to the Word
of God ! That alone will set you right again."
Thus runs Zwingli's will.